THE MEANING OF THE
SACRAMENTAL SYMBOLS

The Meaning of
the Sacramental Symbols

Answers to Today's Questions

Klemens Richter

Translated by Linda M. Maloney

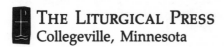
THE LITURGICAL PRESS
Collegeville, Minnesota

The Meaning of the Sacramental Symbols: Answers to Today's Questions was originally published by Verlag Herder under the title: Klemens Richter, *Was die sakramentalen Zeichen bedeuten. Zu Fragen aus der Gemeinde von heute.* © 1988 Verlag Herder.

Cover design by Joshua Jeide, O.S.B.

1	2	3	4	5	6	7	8	9

Library of Congress Cataloging-in-Publication Data

Richter, Klemens.
    [Was die sakramentalen Zeichen bedeuten. English]
    The meaning of the sacramental symbols : answers to today's questions /
Klemens Richter ; translated by Linda M. Maloney.
      p. cm.
    Translation of: Was die sakramentalen Zeichen bedeuten.
    ISBN 0-8146-1882-0
    1. Sacraments—Catholic Church. 2. Catholic Church—Doctrines.
3. Catholic Church—Liturgy. I. Title.
BX2200.R5213 1990   89-77872
234'.16—dc20   CIP

Contents

A WORD OF INTRODUCTION

Liturgical action depends on symbols because human beings cannot be together and communicate without some kind of encounter in words (verbal symbols) and/or in gestures and actions (nonverbal symbols). All knowledge begins with our senses; this means that an encounter with God is only possible by means of sensible signs. The decisive sign of God's presence is Jesus Christ, the central sacrament of the divine salvific will, the first and fundamental sacrament. In him and in his actions we are given an image, a picture of God. Since Christ, by sending the Holy Spirit, continues to live and work in his Church, the Church is a basic symbol of that saving will: It is a fundamental sacrament. And so the Church's activity, its basic obligation to proclaim the faith (*martyria:* witness), to celebrate the faith (*liturgia:* worship), and to do what the faith calls us to do (*diakonia:* service)—all this is, as a whole, a sacramental action in symbols through which the coming of the reign of God is realized. It follows that all the actions of worship can be called sacramental, for every liturgical sign is intended, in the last analysis, to help us encounter God, and to make possible a liturgy that is a dialogue between God and human persons. The term "sacramental symbols" thus covers not only the sacraments but all celebrations in which God is worshiped.

The encounter with God in the liturgy, then, is not only expressed in symbols; the celebration as a whole is a symbol in which the memory of God's saving deeds in the past becomes present salvation for the community through Christ's action in the Holy Spirit. This means that being-a-symbol is constitutive for liturgy. And so it is not simply a matter of understanding individual symbols; we must comprehend the whole liturgical celebration as a symbolic action, a symbol of the presence of God that can be experienced only in this way in the liturgy or else not at all.

This book was inspired by questions that have been answered by the author over a period of years in the periodical *Christ in der Gegenwart (The Christian Today)*. It makes no claim to completeness. Some are questions that continually arise in our Church and parish communities, as we try to understand the whole liturgy as a symbolic action; others relate to the carrying out of the liturgical symbols, whose renewal ought to have as a result "that they express more clearly the holy things which they signify [and that] Christian people, as far as possible, should be able to understand them with ease and to take part in them fully, actively, and as befits a community." (Vatican Council II, Constitution on the Sacred Liturgy [*Sacrosanctum Concilium;* hereafter *SC*], 21). This little volume is dedicated to this goal of liturgical renewal.

My thanks are extended to those with whom I am most closely united in this effort, my colleagues and co-workers in the Department of Liturgical Studies at the University of Münster, especially Brigitte Mülder.

Klemens Richter

LITURGY AS EXPRESSIVE
AND SYMBOLIC ACTION

1

"Sign" or "Symbol"?

The words "sign" and "symbol" are very often used in the same sentence and spoken in the same breath. Is there any difference between them, or do they mean the same thing? Is "sign" just an English synonym for "symbol"?

In ordinary speech the two words are in fact nearly interchangeable. In the natural sciences especially, they are used to mean the same thing. And in our everyday language the idea of "symbol" can even be used in such a way that it expresses two completely contradictory notions: On the one hand an extremely important action is called "a truly symbolic gesture," while on the other hand something meaningless is described as "merely symbolic."

Originally, "symbol" meant "the broken halves of a whole," the two parts of a divided object. When the two halves were brought together (Greek *symballein)*, the symbol could serve as a means of recognition: The person who had one part thus proved that she or he was a messenger, designated host, or partner in an agreement. A later development of this custom was the seal, since a seal and its impression together made up a whole. That is why confirmation, for example, could be described as a "sealing." So a symbol is a sign consisting of two parts, in such a way that the whole is only visible when the two halves are brought together. But

often signs are only called symbols if their meaning is of special importance. Thus every symbol is a sign, but not every sign is a symbol. In the language of religion and theology it is frequently the case that the concept of "symbol" is reserved for the signs of faith, that is, for those signs which have, in addition to their superficial, natural meaning, another and supernatural meaning that is only accessible to faith (P. Harnoncourt).

For people in the ancient world, a symbol was not only the visible part of a whole. In the symbol, the visible reality of the whole was present, although in its entirety it remained invisible. So "symbol" means "a whole reality" insofar as it presents itself through the symbol.

Since the Middle Ages, Western Christianity has been almost completely oblivious to this way of seeing things. The question of whether Christ is really or symbolically present in the Eucharistic species could not have arisen in antiquity, because the whole reality was evident in the symbol. A genuine and original symbol thus "does not stand for something different, something which it 'means.' It is not a substitute; it is really what it represents and means. To put it more radically, 'it communicates itself and preserves itself by presenting and showing itself' " (A. Wucherer-Huldenfeld). Only when people began to think of symbol as "no longer meaning a reality that presents itself, but instead a weakened sort of reality . . . could this kind of question arise and lead to a controversy about the Eucharist" (A. Adam/R. Berger).

So in speaking of the liturgy as sign we can say that it not only points to something else, like every sign, but that it makes a reality present. Thus "the concept of symbol has a deeper, more comprehensive sense, because it intends to present and describe a real means of communication between God and humanity under the aspect of sign." In this way it signifies "the indivisible joining and commingling of a human, this-worldly aspect and a divine component" (T. Schneider).

This is especially clear in Jesus Christ, who according to the repeated testimony of Sacred Scripture is in his humanity the Word of God (see John 1:1, 14; 1 John 5:7; Rev 19:13) and the image of God (see 2 Cor 4:4; Col 1:15; cf. also Wis 7:26), the sign of God's presence in the world. The First Letter of John begins: "That which was from the beginning, which we have heard, which we have seen with our eyes, which we have looked upon and touched with our hands, [this we proclaim to you]: . . . the Word of life." What is decisive for Christian liturgy is that Christ has made salvation dependent on signs: "The one who eats my flesh and drinks my blood has eternal life" (John 6:54). "Unless one is born of water and the Spirit, [that one] cannot enter the kingdom of God" (John 3:5). A further reason why liturgy is only possible in signs—verbal (those made up of words) as well as nonverbal, because words are also signs, which makes it very imprecise to talk of "word and sign"—is grounded in human nature: communication between people, too, is only possible in and through signs.

So it is not of fundamental importance whether we use the concept of "sign" or of "symbol." The important thing is to be clear about what these words necessarily mean in the context of liturgy.

2

What Is the Difference Between Sacraments and Other Sacramental Symbols?

As we pointed out in the introductory remarks, the concept of "sacramental sign" can be applied not only to the sacraments but to all worship celebrations. From that point of view it seems rather undesirable to distinguish between administration of sacraments, meaning the seven sacraments in the narrow sense of the term, and sacramental celebrations, by which we refer to liturgical actions not pertaining directly to the seven sacraments, such as the celebration of Christian burial or various blessings. Both sacraments and sacramentals contain "a visible and an invisible component; that is, there is a reality that is accessible to human experience and perception, which nevertheless is ultimately beyond human grasp and remains a mystery. What is visible, apparent, and accessible is a sign of what is invisible, hidden, and mysterious" (R. Kaczynski). The distinction between sacraments and sacramentals was first proposed in the Middle Ages as part of a process of theological systematizing. But the early Church applied the word *sacramentum* to the whole of God's saving activity. This word was used to translate the New Testament Greek term *mysterion* ("mystery"—cf. Rom 16:25-26). *Mysterion* could be used to refer to God's plan of salvation as a whole as well as the several phases of realization of that plan, whose center is Jesus Christ. Christ is the real mystery of divine saving action, a fact which in itself makes clear that the translation of this concept with the English "mystery" is incapable of conveying the meaning of this idea in its fullness.

Since Christ is the central sacrament of salvation, and since he continues his work in the sacrament of the Church, the Church's whole liturgical activity can be called sacramental:

> Some of the liturgical celebrations are called sacraments in a special sense, namely those in which [the Church]—and ultimately, of course, Christ himself as he lives and acts in the Church—makes present and celebrates the Christ-mystery from incarnation and birth to death and resurrection. In addition, the Old Testament forms of cultic expression, which are most often interpreted typologically as pointing toward Christ and the Church, [see ch. 15 below], are called sacraments. The Church's magisterium, using forms of expression that have been common since the early Scholastic Period, employs the number seven and the technical term "sacrament" to refer to those liturgical symbols and symbolic actions that in their substance go back to Jesus and that produce and communicate those effects peculiar to them "always and universally, so far as this depends on God" *(ex opere operato)*. In this way the ancient Church's concept of "sacrament" is restricted to only a few liturgical actions (R. Kaczynski).

But the whole substance of the Church's sacramental life cannot be reduced to these seven sacraments, for the Christ-mystery is also celebrated in other liturgical symbols. "These liturgical symbols and symbolic actions, developing in the course of history 'through the power of the Church's intercessory prayer' *(ex opere operantis ecclesiae)* were summarily described as sacramentals" (R. Kaczynski). But in both cases it is a matter of the one life of the Church, and of the Church's sacramental activity, so that the distinction made by theologians for systematic purposes between sacraments and sacramentals is not necessarily helpful for liturgical action. For both sacraments and sacramentals are visible signs of invisible grace which make effective in the community the saving actions of the Father, mediated through Christ in the Holy Spirit.

Too much fixation on the seven sacraments narrows our vision of the breadth of God's saving activity. The sacrament of reconciliation offers one example. Certainly, God's reconciling activity in the Christian community is concentrated in a special way in the sacramental celebration of penance. But we should not overlook the fact that the manifold possibilities for reconciliation between God and human persons in other liturgical celebrations have too often been lost sight of, as a result of a too-exclusive concentration on the sacrament itself (see ch. 33 below). But it has always been the faith of the Church that sins are forgiven, for example, through works of charity, through faithful listening to God's Word, through the confession of sins that is part of nearly all liturgical celebrations—as well as through special liturgical celebrations of penance, as long as those sins do not have such weight that the magnitude of guilt is cause for exclusion from the community's Eucharist.

It follows that, in concert with the Church of the early centuries, we can refer to all liturgical symbols as sacraments, sacramentals, or sacramental symbols. The proposed schema for the Constitution on the Liturgy at Vatican II had suggested the removal of the conceptual distinction between sacraments and sacramentals, but this proposal was defeated on the basis of that Western theology that still stems from the Middle Ages. In contrast, the Eastern Church has held fast to the concept of *mysterion,* and, as a result, makes no distinction between sacraments and sacramentals.

3

Can We Understand Symbols?

In articles and lectures on liturgy and liturgical reform we hear and read again and again that modern people, saturated with the world-image presented by natural science, simply cannot understand symbols and signs anymore. And the question of our capability for liturgy is closely bound up with that of our capability for dealing with symbols. For those who have no access to the meaning of symbols, liturgical celebration is simply impossible.

This is not a new question. A quarter of a century ago, just after the Constitution on the Liturgy had been accepted (December 4, 1963), Romano Guardini, in a letter of April 1, 1964, to the Third Liturgical Congress in Mainz, asked in the sharpest tone possible:

> Could it be that the liturgical action, and with it all that "liturgy" means, is so bound up with history—ancient, medieval, or baroque—that, to be really honest, we need to abandon it entirely? Should we not come to the realization that people in an age of industry, technology, and the sociological structures demanded by them, are simply no longer capable of liturgical activity? And, instead of talking about renewal, should we not rather consider how the sacred mysteries might be celebrated in order that these people of today, as they really are, can be present in and to those mysteries?

Adolf Adam was quite right when he wrote in his book *Grundriß der Liturgie* (Fundamentals of Liturgy):

> It is clear from the context that Guardini is not questioning the liturgy in its fundamental aspect as mystery of the gift of salvation and the glorification of God. He is primarily concerned with the "liturgical ac-

19

tion" which human beings must carry out in a physical-symbolic manner, which they must "see," and into which they must insert their whole personalities.

The question concerning the capability of modern people for dealing with signs and symbols led, even at that time, to a broad-based discussion, in the course of which the Benedictine Burkhard Neunheuser from Maria Laach pointed out that this is not only a problem for Christians:

> Are there people today who are able to look at a work of art, to listen to a symphony, to gaze at a landscape, to celebrate a festival, and all of it not only as passive spectators but as active participants and with inner appropriation, in the emotions of the heart, in silence, with astonishment, exaltation, and enthusiasm, in solemn resonance, with all their strength—and are they able to find the appropriate expression for the movement of their hearts, the expression of high festival, of praise and glory, in community with others who share their feelings?

So what we are dealing with here is not a problem that was created by liturgical reform. For in the same letter Guardini writes that even people in the nineteenth century were no longer capable of liturgical action:

> For them, the religious attitude was something purely individual and interior—which then, as "liturgy," simply added an official and public character of celebration. But the meaning of liturgical action was lost in the process. What believers did was not really liturgical; it was a private, interior act surrounded by ceremony—quite often accompanied by a feeling that the ceremony was a distraction from the real action.

In contrast to private religious acts, liturgical action is a community act. Thus, an aptitude for liturgy involves not only a capability for symbols and signs but necessarily an ability to be in community (see ch. 6 below).

Although it may be true that we in our time are colder toward symbols than were people of another age, nevertheless, our industrial culture has also produced a wealth of symbols: Flags are hoisted and torn down, hair is worn long or short as a demonstration of something. It may say something about the difficulties in this area that there have seldom been so many books written about signs and symbols as in the last few years—and quite a few of these, by the way, come from Protestants. Since the beginnings of the liturgical movement and especially since Guardini's book *Sacred Signs* (1924–25), liturgical symbols have repeatedly been the objects of pastoral-liturgical consideration. In addition, it is now a matter of conviction in the fields of sociology, psychology, and psychoanalysis that the use of rites and symbols is a necessary aspect of being human. If we close ourselves off from nonverbal signs, we get sick.

4

Has Liturgical Reform Killed Symbolic Language?

It is often asked, if not simply stated as a fact, whether liturgical reform as a whole has not impoverished our symbolic language.

Balthasar Fischer, one of the most important participants in the reform movement worldwide, is convinced that

> the slogan about the recent Catholic liturgical reform's being an enemy of symbolic language is a superficial and unjustified blanket condemnation that falsely attaches to the reform itself what many of the "consumers" who make use of the reformed rites have—unfortunately—made of them. Where the reform is carried out as it was intended, the long-celebrated treasure of "nonverbal communication" in the Catholic liturgy is greatly strengthened.

He sees a major gain in the realm of liturgical symbols as a result of eliminating some signs, making others more concise, and introducing or reintroducing still others.

Let me give an example of a gain achieved by eliminating a sign that no longer yielded any meaning: Before the reform it was customary for the priest, at the concluding doxology of the Eucharistic prayer, to make the sign of the cross with the host three times over the chalice and then three times between the chalice and the edge of the altar. These six signs of the cross could only be explained allegorically (see ch. 15 below) as representing the wounds of Christ, for example, or as a sign that the Crucified desires to gather people to himself from the four corners of the world. As a result, there was a lot of discussion in the Middle Ages about the number of signs of the cross that should be made. The elimination of this scarcely intelligible sign is surely a plus.

In addition, a number of symbols were tightened up by being reduced in some way. Here we might mention the many genuflections or kissings of the altar during the Mass. When the priest kissed the altar each time before turning to the people, the original function of this gesture as a greeting to the altar and a taking leave of it was no longer visible. Therefore, there remains only one kiss of greeting and one on leaving the altar.

What is decisive, however, is the fact that vestigial symbols have been revived and new symbols have been created. Consider, for example, the celebration of the Eucharist with the priest facing the people. Certainly the old method of celebrating with the priest's back to the congregation was also a meaningful symbol: It symbolized their mutual turning toward the one Lord. But at the same time, this form promoted the false notion that the Mass was something the priest "did" and at which the laity "were present," or "attended," as we in fact used to say. But when the priest faces the people, the priestly function of presiding and acting as host to the community assembled around the altar-table again comes to the fore and corresponds to the action at the Last Supper. It is much the same with the symbol of imposition of hands. At reconciliation and at the anointing of the sick this sign, as a laying of the hands on the head of the penitent or of the sick person, was scarcely discernible. The grill in the confessional permitted only an extending of the hand toward the penitent, which she or he could not even see. Today in the reconciliation room—unless there is still a confessional grill to prevent it—an imposition of hands is again part of the ritual. And at the anointing of the sick as well the imposition of both hands before the anointing, which had disappeared (probably for reasons of prudery), has been reintroduced and is obligatory. This symbol, of course, can only "speak" if the symbolic language in it is clearly expressed: in a silent, perceptible, and not-too-brief laying on of the hands.

An example of a newly created sign is the signing of the forehead of the one being baptized by the parents and sponsors, a sign that is immediately understood and requires no explanation. Practice has shown that the parents and sponsors recognize what this signing means.

We should also recall the renewal of a symbol that has now made itself felt throughout the whole Church: the symbol of the intelligible word. Of course, liturgical Latin also had a symbolic character:

> [It] was a sign of the unapproachability of what is here celebrated; of its elevation beyond the ordinary. But there still remained the great objection that it is precisely the *word* which is given to human beings, not to conceal, but to reveal, and that Christian liturgy, of all things, is governed in its entirety by the command to proclaim a message and to assemble all into a commonly understood prayer (B. Fischer).

So we cannot speak of any loss of symbolic language when the basic principles of liturgical reform are really filled with life. It is a question for parish communities, but especially for priests, how they will deal with the fullness of signs.

5

Do Symbols
Have to Be Learned?

Quite a few people today think that the symbols and gestures of the liturgy are often not understood or, to put it another way, that they do not express what they are supposed to signify: the faith of the assembled community.

There are special problems with those symbols that the participants encounter only in the liturgical actions and nowhere else. Besides symbols that by their very nature serve to illuminate our existence, we use others that have acquired their meaning through historical tradition. The fact that the meaning of such symbols has to be learned is not necessarily a defect; it can even add to their value. Sociologists tell us that a newcomer who enters into a large group learns during the socialization process, among other things, what meaning the group attaches to its symbols. Those who do not know these symbols, or who know them but neither accept the meaning attached to them nor attempt to conform to the behavioral demands they pose, are by that very fact shown to be nonmembers. Social symbols, and especially religious signs, are indispensable for separating those who belong to a group from those who do not. If the symbols disappear the contours of the group are blurred, and it enters into a stage of dissolution.

What creates the most confusion and rejection in the liturgy today is the accumulation and the constant repetition of certain signs. Heinrich Rennings has pointed out that in the Missal that was used before 1970 the celebrant had to genuflect every two minutes during a celebration lasting half an hour; he had to make a sign of the cross every thirty-five seconds and kiss the altar every three minutes—in all, sixteen genuflections, fifty-two signs of the cross, and ten kisses of the altar. We can hardly blame anyone for thinking that this kind of piling up of signs is unnecessary.

In the effort to create some variety, it sometimes happens that not only the variable liturgical elements are changed but that all the symbols are altered. This kind of alteration can reduce the value of the symbols within the communication process of the celebration (see ch. 20 below), since the meaning of a symbol results from its sameness. Like the standard opening of a television series or the unaltered packaging of a consumer product, ritual elements serve the cause of recognition and function as signals. Beyond mere conscious recognition, they evoke expectations, attitudes, and feelings. Constant elements like these make common celebration easier.

The attachment of symbols to faith is also important. Symbols without faith are ineffective. They cannot replace faith. The visible aspect of a symbol does not reveal its ultimate content.

So the liturgical symbols and liturgy as a whole stand in the closest possible relationship to faith and theology. In the liturgy, the content of faith and of theology, the mystery of salvation that runs through the whole of human history, is again and again made present and effective under sacred signs. Therefore, the liturgical actions themselves are symbols of the faith of the community. This relationship between liturgy, faith, and theology has important consequences for theology itself and also for the liturgical symbols. Prior to any attempt at speculative and systematic penetration, theology must first orient itself by consulting Sacred Scripture as witness of Christian tradition, and also the other witnesses, namely, the texts and actions of the liturgy: in other words, the liturgical symbols. And this is true not only of those symbols that are regarded as essential but for the whole sweep of a liturgical celebration (see ch. 9 below). Thus the fact that the liturgy is an important source for theology is yet another reason why it is necessary to learn the symbolic language of liturgy.

6

Can Symbols Be Used
for Liturgical Education?

It is clear enough that at the present time there are difficulties involved in dealing with liturgical symbols. Does it necessarily follow that these symbols should become a focus of liturgical education? A basic openness to comprehending symbols is part of human education in general and precedes liturgical education as such. Anyone who cannot forgive and ask for forgiveness, accept gifts and give them, give thanks, celebrate, and share a meal with others, will not be able to appreciate liturgical symbols either.

But undoubtedly the understanding and carrying out of sacramental symbols are among the essential elements of liturgical education. Here we can again refer to Romano Guardini, who was concerned from the outset for a wholistic introduction into liturgy and less about intellectual transmission of ideas. For that reason, his basic questions were, "What is the essence of a liturgical attitude? What must be the makeup of a human person and of a community if they are to be properly present within the liturgy?" His reflections were directed in the first instance toward an education that would make people adept in the use of symbols and in community life.

Since liturgical action involves the whole person, the body must be understood as a symbol, the only locus in which the spiritual can express itself. Every kind of one-sided spiritualization must be avoided. The liturgy demands the whole human person:

> Its fulfillment does not result in extracting the praying persons from their bodiliness. On the contrary: they are . . . increasingly human.

27

That is to say, in liturgical action the bodiliness of human persons is more and more deeply internalized, penetrated by spirit; and the human soul expresses itself more and more fully in its embodiedness.

But if the whole person is drawn into the liturgy in attitude, gesture, and action, other symbols acquire a new value within the liturgy: "The body's means of expression, its members and movements, are insufficient to reveal the fullness of what is in the soul. Human beings expand their possibilities by drawing objects from the environment into the realm of their own bodies." Thus objective, spatial, and temporal means of expression are drawn into and included in the fundamental body-soul relationship. A precondition for this is the recognition that all external objects can be symbols:

> A symbol arises when something interior and spiritual finds expression through something exterior and physical . . . . It is necessary . . . that what is interior should translate itself into what is exterior. . . . But it is a further characteristic of symbols in the fullest sense that they are clearly delimited, so that this form of expression cannot equally well represent something different.

This symbol must also be naturally adapted to its purpose, that is, we must not do violence to the thing itself: It must permit the interpretation without being forced. "Whenever we have to say: 'this used to be so and so . . . that really means such and such . . . we ought to recognize this or that within this symbol,' then the object itself no longer speaks to us, and we are asking the faithful to give it an artificial voice." But when people have been forced to put their own meaning into the symbols, a common understanding of the liturgical action is no longer possible, since on the one hand mistakes in translation can lead to wrong ideas, and on the other hand we have left the way wide open for an individualistic and privatistic interpretation based on feeling.

This brings us also to the subject of aptness for community life, because the liturgy is *not* about personal uplift toward God but is a mutual action of the assembled community. Thus, the liturgy demands that we be prepared to share the lives of others and to take their suffering and their hopes as our own.

This also involves an education in objectivity. The liturgical symbols are objective because here a spiritual content that is to be understood by everyone is molded into a form we can apprehend with our senses. The liturgy is also objective to the extent that it expresses basic Christian beliefs, before which subjective feelings must give way. It is thus the duty of liturgical education to draw people from subjective narrowness to objective breadth, but at the same time to help them learn to think with the Church. For Guardini, thinking as and with the Church (*sentire cum ecclesia*) is necessary because liturgy, the concrete here-and-now celebration of a particular congregation, is always at the same time the liturgy of the whole Church.

It is thus obvious that a conscious and knowledgeable performance of the liturgical signs is an essential element of liturgical education.

7

Is Sensuousness Constitutive for Liturgy?

Anyone who finds the connection of sensuousness with divine worship extraordinary might be reminded of one of the weightiest attacks on the whole liturgical reform of Vatican Council II, made in a book by an atheist psychoanalyst, A. Lorenzer, entitled *The Bookkeepers' Council* (Frankfurt, 1981) and subtitled "The Destruction of Sensuousness." Has the renewal of our liturgy really destroyed its sensuousness or—to use a phrase that may be less objectionable although it is really the same thing—its bodiliness, or accessibility to the senses? There is plenty of talk at least about a loss of symbolic quality; it comes from people who think that, as the liturgy now stands, it is words alone that count and, moreover, that those words are too demanding or abstruse and cannot be rightly understood (see ch. 4 above).

Very much like Guardini, the Lutheran theologian Wilhelm Stählin remarks that "anything that is not in bodily form is not really on this earth; the body is the locus of realization." He continues: "In this reality called 'body' our particular destiny is lived out. Nothing happens to us that does not also happen to our bodies, and whatever really and deeply touches us is experienced 'in our bodies.' " It is evident that this is also true of the liturgy, for the mystery of God, the divine saving action, encounters people in bodily form in Jesus Christ. In him it has become visible, audible, and tangible. Only through signs that express this fact can people come in contact with salvation. Only thus can they take hold of it and make it their own. "Human nature and the nature of revelation call for sensible forms," because otherwise there would be a danger "of losing ourselves in mystical states of the soul, in cold ideologies, or in ethical concerns. That a disappearance of symbols and the lack of physical event really leads to verbalism and moralism is most clearly evident from the present state of Catholic liturgies," writes the liturgist Jakob Baumgartner.

The symbolic quality of the liturgy thus touches all the senses. However, in the Western Church there was a very early tendency, evident even in Augustine (d. 430), to reduce it to the senses of hearing and seeing. But all the senses should be included, for example, the sense of smell in the use of incense; the sense of taste in enjoyment of the gifts of bread and wine; the sense of touch in feeling the water in baptism, the chrism in confirmation, the oil and the imposition of the hand in the anointing of the sick, and embracing or shaking hands at the sign of peace.

Since all the senses should be addressed in the liturgy, the conciliar description of the liturgy as *signa sensibilia,* translated into English as "signs perceptible to the senses" (*SC* 7), is really a tautology—a repetition, since signs are always perceptible to the senses.

Although at the present time great efforts are being made to integrate the body into our lifestyle, in the realm of faith we continue to act like Puritans in many respects. It is symptomatic of this state of affairs that even the latest discussions of the Eucharistic celebration scarcely touch the question of physical engagement but have a lot to say about the role of the word. And yet, Jesus' command to his disciples regarding the central liturgical celebration of the Christian community, the Eucharist, was "Do this in memory of me."

> It was not: "consider, praise, proclaim, talk about what has happened," but rather: "Do it!" Accordingly, liturgy is essentially poetry, deed, action, performance. Certainly, it is also deed as word, but not only that. Liturgy as an activity appropriate to human beings takes into account all aspects of our nature: our worldliness and bodiliness, our temporality and community. It approves the "poetry" of objects and of bodies, of place and time; in short, the poetry of the human being in his or her totality (J. Baumgartner).

It says a lot about our understanding of total human action in the Eucharist when even students of theology, in answer to the question of what the essential Eucharistic symbols are, say, "bread and wine." We are talking about the celebration of a meal, for the sacrifice of the Mass is in the form of a meal. But where and how, in our current Eucharistic celebrations, is it visible and clearly recognizable that this is a community meal? The usual method of distributing communion to the people as they come forward in two rows would scarcely make anyone think of a meal; a host that neither looks nor tastes like bread does not serve that function either, and the cup is not offered at all—primarily for "practical" reasons.

Dieter Emeis notes, concerning this necessary learning process, that there is a discrepancy "between, on the one hand, the body-soul unity of the human person which is described in nearly every anthropology and, on the other, a scarcely developed attention to the body as visible and tangible expression of inner attitudes, convictions, movements, and expectations." He mentions, as a deficit of the most recent tradition, that the sacraments are primarily regarded as means to grace and thought of from the point of view of validity as regards the minister and the recipient. We are still too-little conscious of the fact that the human body itself is a symbol—in fact, *the* symbol—through which God reaches out to human beings in the liturgy. Only

> when we have experienced our normal eating (and drinking) as symbolic, can we also carry out the Eucharistic eating (and drinking) as symbolic action: as a reception of nourishment and strength drawn from Jesus Christ's surrender of himself to death, which are given to us in order that we may live from them. A devout Communion, then, does not merely demand mental attentiveness; the attention of the spirit serves the attention of the body, in which the invitation to eat (and drink) is experienced as a gift for the sake of our life. Education of the body, in this context, means an upbringing such that one can, at least occasionally, eat (and drink) with attention and devotion, in such a way that these actions are recognized as a basic bodily experience of the human person.

The liturgical reform has made an effort to permit the essential symbols to appear anew, in their sentience and bodiliness. The fact that this is not mere theory is clear when one regards liturgical celebrations in the Third World, which literally burst with sensuousness. In the praxis of our own communities and parishes, the translation of this demand into liturgical action has still not been carried out very often. For the most part, the participants in the liturgy do not give enough thought to their bodiliness. It seems as if we are ashamed to accept ourselves as bodily creatures at a liturgical celebration. Often a pure interiority is still regarded as the ideal. It is precisely the most "pious" people who need to have explained to them that prayer involving the whole body need not be the opposite of personal devotion. Liturgy really begins with the fact that we are totally present, with body and soul. But that is not the case when abstract intellect and purposive will smother everything else. If liturgy has something to do with feasting and joy, all the senses should be engaged: hearing, seeing, smelling, tasting, and feeling.

8

*Why Are Our Celebrations
So Barren of Sensible Qualities?*

There are a number of obstacles to an adaptation of our worship in the direction of bodiliness. Some of them appeared centuries ago, while others have only become apparent in our own time. Let me mention a few of them.

The word, which is itself a sign, has fundamental importance for liturgy. However, it began very early to be overvalued in the West, in contrast to the Churches of the East, which remained in principle more open to visual factors. An indication of this is the interpretation of divine revelation as a purely verbal event, whereas, in fact, the concept of revelation itself is taken directly from the visual realm. This corresponds to the words of Jesus in which he calls blessed those who see and hear (see Matt 13:16; cf. 11:4). In this regard, Vatican Council II emphasized repeatedly that revelation does not consist merely in words but also in the deeds of God and Christ. Accordingly, "evangelization" is not only a proclamation of the Word, but also the celebration of the liturgy and its application in life. Although Catholics, in contrast to the Reformers, emphasized the role of symbolism, this did not prevent them from giving primary respect to the word, as is clearly revealed by the former text of the precept of the Church: the people (are obligated to "hear" Mass.) *celebrate*

> The urgently needed reemphasis on the word and its sacramental effectiveness, which because of a reaction against the Reformers had almost been forgotten in Catholic theology, was stated in principle by the Council and carried out in practice by the liturgical reform. But

in its concrete realization it has frequently led to an inflation of words, to an insistent tone of information, if not indoctrination, and to an urgency of motivation and flat-footed moralism that is often quite narrowly subjective. This is one of the reasons for the fanatic resistance of traditionalist groups and for the apparent unease of others (E. J. Lengeling).

Since the Middle Ages, the interest of systematic theology in particular has been concentrated on the effectiveness of the signs and thus on all those things, and those things only, that guarantee the validity of the sacraments in extreme cases. This necessarily led to impoverishment and spiritualization, since it was primarily a question of guaranteeing validity by means of a ritual correctly performed. The objective accomplishment of the rite was in the foreground, not infrequently verging on magical interpretation, while the liturgical celebration was no longer regarded as a process in which the faith of the whole person was articulated and embodied.

The intellectualism of Western theology still supplies no basis in which an understanding for embodied liturgy can take good root and grow. It is not simply a question of "getting it through one's head" but also of grasping it in one's heart. Thus even today, according to a recent statement by pastoral theologian and religious educator Dieter Emeis, in most of the proposals for sacramental catechesis

> there is a lot more said about what the various sacraments are than about how they are celebrated. . . . The fact that in many suggested forms of catechesis a symbolic perception and way of acting is not decisively promoted is due not only to an orientation toward the essence rather than toward the celebration of the sacraments. It is evidently not sufficiently acknowledged in the analysis of preconditions for catechesis that we, who live in a world shaped by modern science and technical knowledge, are handicapped in our ability to recognize symbols and to communicate symbolically.

Emeis therefore calls for emotional and psychomotor processes of learning, since it is not the least of the tasks of a Christian community to learn how to differentiate itself from its environment by means of a culture of symbols that involve the whole person.

Modern individualism is also a danger for a total performance of liturgy. Only those who are prepared to trust and cooperate with other people and not merely to celebrate "their own" worship service are really capable of liturgy.

> In our Western lifestyle, the clearly dominant values are achievement, goal-directed activity, thought and will, reasons and calculation; other layers of our being remain underdeveloped. Out of this situation arises a feeling of frustration, unease, and disappointment. The liturgy reform, too, was carried out primarily by intellectuals and bears the traces of this impoverishment. For a worship service to regain its expressive power it will be necessary that it reclaim its character as event, as an action of gesture and symbols, in short, as a fully human act. The ecstasy of faith—do we still expect to find that in our liturgies? (J. Baumgartner).

These are just some of the obstacles in the way of a reembodiment, a stronger quality of sentience in our worship. But we cannot blame the liturgy for something that has its bases somewhere else. The liturgy can only express in signs what really motivates the assembled community—it must be the genuine expression of its faith. So it is up to each community whether its worship services are full of the delight of the senses or are, instead, rational and boring.

9

What Is Essential?
What Is Secondary?

The decisive, primary, and therefore fundamental sign of the celebration of faith is the assembly of the community itself. For this is where the Church is most clearly present, and thus it is an effective sign, a mystery, the fundamental sacrament (see ch. 2 above). To this essential symbol, the liturgical assembly, are added the essential liturgical actions, the sacraments, as principal signs. In them the turning points in life, basic human situations like birth and table sharing, marriage and entry into office, are given a new quality in Christ. The event itself is represented by signs drawn from daily life: bath, meal, promise, the touch of the hand.

> These signs are not just some kind of images in the pedagogical or poetic sense, in which an invisible event is made evident through symbols and pictorial representations. Instead, what happens here is that an invisible and inaudible gracious event receives its own specification through signs. The sacraments effect what they signify, because they signify it (E. J. Lengeling).

Insofar as the sacramental signs were determined by Christ or by the primitive Church, they should probably not be changed. But we need to try—and this is the duty of liturgical reform (cf. *SC* 33; 59)—to recover the clarity of these indispensable signs so that they can better serve the cause of faith. These signs were, and to some extent still are, distorted: The Eucharistic bread became a little white slice of something that reminds one more of plastic than of basic nourishment; the pouring of water over the one being baptized, as a sign that God washes away his or her entire guilt, was reduced to a few drops of water.

The dividing line between primary (essential) and secondary (less important) signs is not always easy to draw. But what was mentioned above—the liturgical assembly and the sum total of liturgical signs—should be distinguished from the other signs, among which we can again divide those which are more important from those which are less so. Thus the place of the liturgical assembly, the church, is certainly to be counted among the important signs, even though the fundamental reality that is represented and reflected by the Christian church building is the community itself. Since the community and its Eucharist sanctify the building, Christianity for a long time, in its early years, did not bless churches.

Time is another important sign, because it is not a matter of indifference *when* something is celebrated. Through the movement of the sun, which was regarded very early as an image of Christ, the day is divided into parts, and the Liturgy of the Hours was shaped according to that rhythm. It is also divided into weeks, in which the Lord's Day is elevated above all others as the day of the Eucharistic celebration of the whole community. And it is certainly not meaningless that, in the course of the Church's year, Christmas is celebrated at the time of the winter solstice and Easter at the beginning of spring, at least in the Mediterranean basin where Christianity first developed and in the Northern Hemisphere. Certainly there is a problem here for the Southern Hemisphere.

Actions that entered the liturgy at a later period and were given various interpretations are clearly secondary: Among these are candles, incense, vestments, and the colors of the liturgical seasons and feasts. There are also signs, for example, the imposition of hands, which are essential for certain liturgical celebrations such as the ordination of bishops, priests, and deacons; while in other liturgical actions such as the beginning of the baptismal ritual, they are not indispensable.

> While the principal signs were stunted in many ways, the secondary signs often multiplied so much that their power of expression suffered. . . . It often happened that signs were piled on signs for the sheer fun of it, and at the expense of their real function of signifying. A genuine liturgical sign should express and effect what is really happening before the eyes of faith. But when, for example (before the renewal of the liturgy) the celebrant, in blessing the baptismal water,

divided it with his hand and sprinkled it in four directions (east, west, south, and north), this imitative gesture only dramatized what the text was describing at that point: the dividing of the waters of the earth at creation and the four rivers arising from Paradise. But none of this was really happening (E. J. Lengeling).

There is probably no need to give reasons why secondary signs that no longer have any function or can only be explained allegorically (see ch. 15 below) have lost their meaning. In this matter, the reform of the liturgical signs aims at nothing but what Augustine praised in the Christian liturgy, contrasting it with other cults: its simplicity, clarity, and comprehensibility. And that means, particularly in our own time, that both the principal symbols and the secondary signs must be recognizable and comprehensible as such (cf. SC 34; 50). It was a declared aim of liturgical reform that the liturgical signs should again appear in the luster of their true form so that they could also express what they signify. How far this intention has been realized everywhere, however, remains a debated question.

10

Community as Fundamental Symbol

We have already said that the assembly of the community is in itself the fundamental sacramental symbol (see ch. 9 above). It is, in its entirety, the subject and bearer of the liturgical action, for "liturgical services are not private functions, but are celebrations of the Church, which is the 'sacrament of unity,' namely, a holy people united and organized under their bishops" (*SC* 26). This is true in the first instance because, in the sequence of ways in which Jesus Christ is present in the liturgical celebration, according to Jesus' word: "Where two or three are gathered in my name, there am I in the midst of them" (Matt 18:20), the assembly represents the first way in which the Lord is present. Correspondingly, The General Instruction of the Roman Missal says: "Christ is really present to the assembly gathered in his name; he is present in the person of the minister, in his own word, and indeed substantially and permanently under the Eucharistic elements" (GIRM 7). It is not that one manner of the Lord's presence is being contrasted with another; the liturgy is regarded as a dynamic event, a process, which begins with the gathering of those called by God. In them, Christ himself is present.

This in no way contradicts the hierarchic division. Every community needs a leader. And as is common in the secular realm also, the most important actions of the community are carried out symbolically by the leader of the community as its representative. If the celebration of the Eucharist is one of the most central actions of the community, the presider over that community must also be the one who presides at this celebration. It is true, in addition, that the presider acts *in persona Christi*, so that through the person presiding, Christ himself leads the celebration. But in this special function the presider is also part of the assembly. Thus the bishop or priest usually is the one who presides over all liturgical assemblies. Depending on the importance of the particular celebration, the function of presider may also be given to another member of the community.

In any case, in the past other ministries were reserved by Church law—that is, by rules that are subject to change—for clerics. When the former Code of Canon Law stated that all the actions of divine worship could only "be carried out by persons legitimately delegated for that purpose," it completely overlooked the fact that laypeople are "a chosen race, a royal priesthood, a holy nation, God's own people" (1 Pet 2:9; cf. 2:4-5), and that participation in the liturgy "is their right and duty by reason of their baptism" (SC 14). For that reason the Council is consistent when it says that the faithful "should give thanks to God; by offering the Immaculate Victim, not only through the hands of the priest, but also with him" (SC 48).

Those who have been baptized and confirmed thus participate in the priesthood of Christ for the salvation of humankind and to the glory of God (cf. Rev 1:6; Acts 2:24,47; Rom 12:1; Heb 13:15). "Priestly" should be understood in the sense of "sacerdotal," not as "presbyteral." The latter refers to the elder, the leader of a community, the presbyter, or priest. Not only Christians who fulfill a particular ministry but all those assembled are doers of the liturgy. That entitles us also to regard the liturgical assembly of the community as the fundamental symbol within whose liturgical actions, through Christ as the mediator between God and humanity, the other sacramental signs unfold themselves.

11

Why Must Symbols Change?

It was an express aim of the liturgical reform to retrieve the expressive power at least of the essential symbols: "Both texts and rites should be drawn up so that they express more clearly the holy things which they signify. Christian people, as far as possible, should be able to understand them with ease and to take part in them fully, actively, and as befits a community" (SC 21).

The symbols of the liturgical celebration, like the faith itself, are located within a tradition, which for the sake of unity with all generations of believers, has been an essential principle of the liturgy from the beginning. But when God gets involved with people, this community is bound to the creative order which God affirms and establishes, with all its conditions of time and space; but it is also caught up in history. This is the basis for legitimate change in the liturgy and thus also in symbols. If liturgy is bound up with the history of God's saving actions on behalf of God's people, it *has* to change! Thus there is a tension between the tradition that cannot be surrendered on the one hand and the necessary demand for change on the other hand. That is true of signs and symbols as well. But what is changeable, and what is unchangeable? First of all, one thing that is certainly unchangeable is the necessity that the Church should fulfill its mission through sacramental signs. What unites us with earlier generations of believers is not, in the first place, the carrying on of particular individual signs but the fulfillment of the command of Jesus Christ to proclaim his death and resurrection and to witness to his love. To do that in signs that can be understood in the particular time and place is really to preserve the tradition. When outdated signs are not understood, they cannot express what they are supposed to signify—the faith of the assembled community. Anyone who would want to cause the Church to bind itself forever and irrevocably to historically conditioned symbols would be doing it a grave disservice. Such a person should ask him- or herself whether this would not, in the final analysis, be tempting the Church to be untrue to its mission.

Vatican Council II expresses it this way: "With the passage of time, however, there have crept into the rites of the sacraments and sacramentals certain features which have rendered their nature and purpose less clear to the people of today; and hence to that extent the need arises to adjust certain aspects of these rites to the requirements of our times" (*SC* 62). The Council also states the principles according to which this should be done: "The rites should be distinguished by a noble simplicity; they should be short, clear, and unencumbered by useless repetitions; they should be within the people's powers of comprehension, and normally should not require much explanation" (*SC* 34).

In this, the "people's powers of comprehension" are to be given more attention than has heretofore been the case. In this connection we speak nowadays of the inculturation of the liturgy, which must be carried out first of all through use of the mother tongue but also by employment of signs that can be understood in the different nations and cultures. But there should also be regard for the powers of comprehension in individual, concrete communities. We should take note of which signs are understood in different cases, and how they are understood. So it can happen that even in our own country different symbols may develop from community to community. One example of this is the sign of peace (see ch. 44 below). A community in which there is a predominantly individualist idea of the liturgy, or in which those taking part in the liturgy do not know one another, will have more difficulty exchanging the sign of peace than will a community in which the members are more closely united with one another outside the liturgical celebration itself. In the first case, the sign of peace may not be appropriate to the power of comprehension of this particular community. However, we probably should ask whether this community is completely capable of liturgy, since community, or *communio,* with one another is also a precondition for Communion, for common sharing in the meal.

12

Can We Develop New Symbols?

Symbols cannot simply be prescribed if they are to be true to and fit in with the various religious experiences and forms of piety. However, it is a precondition for the validity of any gesture that we first understand the structural laws of the liturgy. Only when that condition is fulfilled can a community begin to consider which actions are appropriate and meaningful in that community's particular context. And at this point we are faced with problems that in earlier periods were simply unknown. As in society as a whole, attitudes and rituals used to develop over long periods of time, and they did so within places and communities that lived under more or less the same conditions throughout. Today that is by no means the case. The rites and symbolic actions at a funeral can be entirely different from community to community or parish to parish, since it may be the case that in a small-town parish the burial itself can be conducted from the church, while in a city parish it may take place far from the parish and perhaps many days after death has occurred. Here individual parishes and communities are required to develop meaningful symbols for their situation, perhaps even to create totally new ones. An unreflective use of what is obsolete can empty the symbol of its meaning and even cause it to mean something completely different.

Thus it is not at all problematic that prayer forms, gestures, and other types of expression are developing in different directions at the present time. It will not be possible to take a kind of objective stand "from above" and from that point of view to determine the one proper action in a particular case. Our communities have at least two important tasks to fulfill in this area: First, they must come to a deeper and deeper recognition of the meaning of the symbolic actions of the liturgy; second, they are called to develop appropriate symbols for themselves and for their various liturgical actions, sometimes even to create them for the first time. This must not be a matter of subjective caprice, for no one may "add, remove, or change anything in the liturgy on his [or her] own authority" (SC 22). It is a fundamental principle that—as SC 23 says—"sound tradition . . . be retained, and yet the way be open for legitimate progress," so that "any new forms adopted should in some way grow organically from forms already existing."

Thus there is no doubt that liturgical piety and its forms of expression are subject to constant change. And that is not something bad; it is a continuing task that requires of each community and the various groups within it a constant reflection on its own forms of worship. Those who are calling for peace and quiet in this area could very easily produce the kind of silence that is the very opposite of a living liturgy and worship.

13

Liturgical Reform and Church Reform Are Inseparable

It is also a fact related to the nature of symbols that a liturgical reform which thinks of the community or parish as subject of the liturgical action is unimaginable without a corresponding reform of the Church itself. We may well ask ourselves whether the rejection "from above" of many requests that in themselves are well justified—such as a Eucharistic prayer adapted for young people or the Swiss canon built around the theme, "God leads the Church" (use of which was denied by the bishops' conference of West Germany)—is not connected with a slowly dawning recognition of the consequences that a renewed liturgy will have for the image of the Church. Even at the risk of misunderstanding, it seems important to consider the following: The postconciliar idea of liturgy presumes that wherever a community assembles, liturgy will be celebrated. This is in contrast to the previous conviction that liturgy is only possible when an ordained minister is available. (There is no question that a priest can celebrate the Eucharist alone, under certain circumstances; but there can be no doubt that in such cases the essential symbol of community is obscured.) Such a weighty change in our understanding of liturgy can clearly not occur without consequences for our whole concept of community.

The whole history of the liturgy plainly shows that a change in the way the faith is understood brings with it a change in the way that faith is celebrated. We need not even think primarily of the Reformation in this connection. When, for various reasons, in the early Middle Ages the presbyter (elder) was increasingly understood as a sacrificing priest, in imitation of the Old Testament sacrificial cult, the result was (not only because of the retention of Latin as the language of the liturgy) that the community was excluded from the liturgy. The people sought a solution through multiple forms of popular piety, many of which were quite far removed from the celebration of the paschal mystery. Since they could no longer be active participants in the Eucharistic celebration and had scarcely any access to Communion, the nearly inescapable consequence was the development of a cult of adoration of the Blessed Sacrament. But when the community is again the subject of the liturgy and participates in the Lord's Supper, it is almost a matter of course that traditional forms of Eucharistic veneration will tend to lose emphasis.

A change in the way the Church is understood also has consequences for the liturgy. If the Church is primarily seen as the body of Christ as it was in the decades immediately before the Council, reform will be more difficult, since any criticism of the Church can be taken as criticism of the Church's head. But if the image of the Church as people of God is preferred, as it was at the Council, changes are much easier to imagine, since a *communio* that is on the road can sometimes lose its way. Should it happen that, in the future, an image of the Church derived from the Holy Spirit should come to the fore, it is possible that it could bring with it a more spontaneous idea of liturgy, in which questions of order and law are less dominant.

There are two crises that will certainly have consequences for the idea of community and for the celebration of the faith: the growing shortage of priests and the shrinking of parish communities, both of which could lead to a closer unity between liturgical community and life setting. If, increasingly, Sunday worship services must be conducted without priests, laypeople will take a more active role in the liturgy, as well as in other areas of Church life. A look at Judaism may be helpful here: the Jews have gotten along for two thousand years without any sacrificial priesthood; the synagogue service is a purely lay liturgy; and the faith is carried on primarily in the family without an authoritative magisterium but through elements of family liturgy; communities of liturgy and life are closely united. Presupposing that we are faced with the transition from a community that is pastored to one that must pastor itself, this situation will also present challenges to our liturgy.

14

The Symbolic Character of the Entire Liturgical Celebration

It was an express aim of the liturgical renewal that the meaning of the Lord's Supper as meal should be restored to the community. Just as a family is probably best represented in its totality when it assembles for a common meal at a family festival, so also in the Eucharistic celebration: Everything that makes up the character of this particular community should be included in its Eucharist. At the beginning of the celebration the events of the week just past should be recounted so that the community will know why it is giving thanks, for whom it ought to pray, and what reasons it has for raising a lament before God. The more vividly this connection between daily life and the Sunday assembly is presented, the more strongly will both forms of Christian life become divine service. The living community experiences its own history with God, and this history is also the content of the Sunday celebration.

Thus it is not so much a question of individual signs, which—even when their meaning is clear—can be quite sterile and ineffective; the important thing is that the worship service in its whole shape and in the way it is performed should be filled by the essence of what it means to be Christian. When this basic condition is fulfilled, the individual signs will also have meaning; in fact, there will be little need to discuss them. To give a secular comparison: When people are convinced of the meaning of the Olympic Games and look forward to them, they will appreciate the opening ceremonies and all their symbolism, even if they might like to have one or another part changed.

So in the Eucharistic celebration: From beginning to end, it should be clear that this common action is a festive meal that is eaten and drunk in grateful joy. If that does not happen, then all the symbols remain isolated and abstract. What takes place may be an act of cultic adoration, but it is not Christian liturgy in its fullest sense as dialogue between God and human persons. Gestures and bodily attitudes indicate clearly what meaning they have for those who are doing them. But we should always ask how far these attitudes correspond to what is demanded by the structural laws of liturgy. For example, we should question whether the Eucharistic prayer, as the proclamation of God's definitive act of salvation, should not be heard standing (as prescribed in The General Instruction of the Roman Missal; see ch. 41 below) rather than kneeling. Even when it is "up to the conference of bishops to adapt the actions and postures described in the order of the Roman Mass to the customs of the people" (GIRM 21), it is still the duty of individual communities to consider what meaning the various signs have for them, so that the whole liturgical celebration will be a sign, on the one hand, of God's saving action in and for God's community and, on the other hand, a sign of the thankfulness and praise of the community toward God.

15

Aren't Sacramental Symbols Often Misinterpreted? Magic, Allegory, and Pretense

Good judgment is needed in making liturgical signs effective for the faithful. "As long as believers' access to an understanding of symbols is made difficult or completely barred because the signs have been obscured, can be understood only in an historical sense, or are not immediately representative, it is futile to complain about resistance to symbols in a technical age" (A. Wucherer-Huldenfeld). So it is part of the transparency and comprehensibility of a sacrament that the faithful can hear the explanatory words. If that is not the case, there is danger that the sacraments will be misunderstood to be a kind of magic. One example of this would be that the Latin words of consecration spoken over the Eucharistic species, *hoc est enim corpus meum,* were bowdlerized into "hocus-pocus" because the Eucharistic words were misunderstood as a magical formula. The impression arose that anyone who could speak these magic words and was permitted to do so could, in a sense, work miracles. It is no wonder that, in light of such a misunderstanding, consecrated hosts were misused—for example, by being placed on wounds to heal them or by being mixed with animal fodder to ward off sickness.

So lack of understanding of a symbol or sign can lead to a false interpretation, in this case to a possible magical misunderstanding. Magic is an attempt to produce beneficial or harmful effects through demonic powers. To exclude such magical misunderstanding, the liturgy always connects explanatory words to the symbolic actions and

51

images. Thus, in the Eastern Churches, every icon should ordinarily have a word written on it. Both together, the image and the explanatory word, permit a real presence, through and in the thing imaged, of the meaning intended by it. We can thus understand why the early Church interpreted the word *symbolum* in a very specific sense: The *credo,* or the fundamental confessions of faith and confessional writings were thought of in a certain sense as signs of recognition within one's own community.

We find a further limitation in the visual images within Western church art that do not represent particular symbols, but instead, by agreement, express religious realities in images. So the shepherd, the lamb, and the fish can stand for Christ, the dove for the soul of someone who has died, and the crown and the palm stand as badges of the martyrs. Obviously, these are not sacramental signs in the specific meaning of the term.

When the meaning attached to a sign is no longer appropriate, when it indicates something totally different from what it is supposed to mean, the liturgical symbol gets covered over by an allegorical interpretation. Especially in the Middle Ages, allegorization became a common principle of interpretation for all the liturgical actions, which in the process were robbed of their true symbolic nature. Allegorization is a principle of interpretation in which a text or action has a meaning different from the one that is immediately apparent. The use of allegory was closely connected with an increasing alienation of the people from the liturgy. Thus, among other things, the succession of actions and the content of the Eucharistic celebration were reinterpreted. There were a number of possibilities. Moral admonitions could be connected with the signs, as when the chasuble was interpreted as a sign of the love of Christ, which encloses all things (moral allegory). Or elements of the Eucharistic celebration could be seen as fulfillment of Old Testament models: The singing of a psalm during the procession with the gifts was said to be a recapitulation of the blowing of the Levites' trumpets during the Temple sacrifices (typological allegory). But for the most part the various actions of the Mass were understood as reminiscences of the life of Jesus. So, for example, the hand washing after the preparation of the gifts, which originally was a necessary cleansing after the reception of natural foodstuffs, came to be seen as an image of Pilate's gesture indicating his guiltlessness: "I wash my hands in innocence." This presented, at the same time, a problematic interpretation of the Mass as sacrifice, for as Pilate had once done, so now the priest sacrificed the body of Christ. To take another example: The five signs of the cross at the conclusion of the Eucharistic prayer represented the five wounds of Christ.

These undoubtedly were inappropriate interpretations. But when the hand washing is seen, as it is today, as a sign of purity of heart, this is a possible appropriate reinterpretation of an action that, at an earlier time, was done for purely practical reasons. Another example: It is appropriate that, in reading the Scriptures, the person reading turns toward the assembly. Before the reform, however, the reader or singer had to turn his or her back to the congregation and proclaim the Gospel (in churches with an east-west orientation) while facing northeast. The allegorical explanation was that the Gospel is proclaimed to the heathen who live in darkness, and they are represented by the North.

A still-greater devaluation and degradation of a sign or an action that formerly had meaning is pretense. Pretense is misleading; it ruins our appreciation for signs and distorts the concept of liturgy. What I mean by pretense is the imitation of an object, as is done in display windows for advertising purposes. Unfortunately, such things have happened in the liturgy also. Such a pretense is the catafalque (no longer permitted) as a sign of the presence of the dead, when in fact the coffin alone should stand there. But spreading out a black cloth in place of the catafalque is to produce a pretense of a pretense. For the same reason, a chalice should not be used to contain the Eucharistic breads being distributed: A chalice is a sign of drinking, not of eating. "We can probably designate as pretense anything that is done in a worship service, even though it has no real function, simply to make it 'valid' " (A. Wucherer-Huldenfeld). Obviously, after the liturgical renewal, there is no longer any place for pretense in our worship.

To prevent these kinds of false interpretations from arising in the future, every community needs to be continually on the alert for the presence in its celebrations of symbols that are really alien to the liturgy.

16

Mystagogy:
Introduction to Sacramental Symbols

Clearly, it is hardly possible to take over Greek concepts in English and use them to designate important aspects of the liturgy. This process seems to have succeeded somewhat in the expression "Eucharistic celebration," but a concept like *mysterium* is not much at home in English, even though it has a very different content than the Latin translation, *sacramentum,* or even the English word "mystery" (see ch. 2 above). We can say something similar about the word "mystagogy."

Originally, mystagogy meant a further introduction of the *mystes,* the initiates, into the experience of celebrating the mysteries. In the second half of the fourth century, then, the concept was increasingly applied to the neophytes, the newly baptized, who were incorporated into the community through baptism, confirmation, and First Eucharist but who apparently were then led more deeply into the Christian life. Since baptism usually took place during the Easter Vigil, this was done primarily through special liturgical celebrations in the course of the week after Easter. This educational process was carried out by means of mystagogical catecheses and homilies.

In the liturgical movement of this century, the concept has been reintroduced to cover, primarily, the notion of liturgical education. We find it very seldom in the postconciliar documents. In a liturgical book on celebrations for the reception of adults into the Church, mystagogy describes a period of introduction and deepening of faith that is supposed to cover the whole Easter season. It is a question of "a complete and cordial acceptance into the community" of believers, which is to cover all aspects, and not only the liturgy. In The Liturgical Education of Candidates for the Priesthood (1979) we read:

> A genuine introduction or mystagogy must above all lay the foundations on which the whole liturgical life is built: the history of salvation, the paschal mystery of Christ, the true nature of the Church, the presence of Christ in the liturgical actions, the hearing of the Word of God, the spirit of prayer, adoration, and thanksgiving, the expectation of the Lord's return.

Here what is at issue is really more than teaching: The heart of the matter is genuine liturgical celebration as such. When the concept of "mystagogy" is used today in a wide variety of different contexts, what is frequently thought of is the homily at Mass, which deals with the texts and actions of the Eucharistic celebration itself and thus may often replace preaching on the Scriptures (so GIRM 41). Quite clearly, this is also the case for other liturgical celebrations such as, for example, baptism or marriage. But there is also talk of a "mystagogical liturgy," which educates through a correct celebration. The idea behind this is appropriate, namely, that an introduction into liturgy and an understanding of it results from personal experience with worship services that convincingly express faith and strengthen it and that establish a successful connection between the community's worship and its Christian life. Of course, that means that everything the liturgy intends is also fully realized.

To give a few examples: The presence of the risen Lord must really be experienced so that the liturgical celebration becomes an encounter with the resurrection; joy must arise out of this experience and be visible in the liturgy as well; the celebration must really be a celebration and not a loveless succession of texts and rites; the whole person must be caught up bodily in it; the liturgy must be credible in itself and correspond to the real life of the community.

Anyone who has lived such an experience in and with the liturgy knows what a mystagogical liturgy is. Making an effort to achieve such celebrations should really be a matter of course. In some of the worship services at Catholic conferences, or in Taizé, the result is almost tangible. And it is certainly not saying too much if we note that, in the long run, only this kind of mystagogical liturgy will be able to support individuals and communities. No matter how much effort is made in liturgical education—and certainly, liturgy will always require a certain amount of explanation—people do not "learn" liturgy by studying but by a worthy and dignified celebration of worship.

17

"Expression" or *"Symbol"*?

In the most recent reflections on liturgical theology it is simply presupposed that liturgical action is the work of the whole human person. Romano Guardini had already taken this pont of view in his little book *Sacred Signs* (trans. by Grace Branham, St. Louis, 1955): "Doing is basic; it includes the whole human person, with all his creative powers. It is the outcome in action of the child's own experience, of his own understanding, of his own ability to look and see." There are two fundamental questions here: What is being expressed, and how is it being expressed? So it is a question, on the one hand, of the content of the liturgy and of faith and, on the other hand, of the expressive dimension of the human person.

In the new *Handbuch der Liturgiewissenschaft (Gottesdienst der Kirche 3*, Regensburg, 1987) (*Handbook of Liturgical Studies: The Church's Worship 3*) there is, consequently, less said about sacramental signs and more about divine worship as an activity of human expression. In fact, human existence as a whole is expression, and human beings fulfill their own being in expressing themselves. Thus A. Ronald Sequeira writes:

> To understand correctly the symbolic character of liturgical expression, we need to keep in mind that human expression is always directed to another. When, for example, two lovers embrace, they experience their love in the very fact that it is directed from each to the other. The embrace is only an imperfect sign of it; and yet it is a symbol of love and expresses the fact that each of the lovers is concerned, not for him-or herself, but for the other. In this sense, genuine expression is always goalless. The lover does not intend to accomplish anything, to possess

anything; she or he desires, instead, to surrender, i.e., each expresses him- or herself as a lover. So we can also say that a believing Christian expresses his or her loving surrender in the liturgy. This expression in worship will also remain inadequate; nevertheless, it is a symbol of the fullness of faith, which cannot be separated from the fullness of the human person. For to the extent that the human person is the being that is directed toward God, the celebration of the liturgy is a form of symbolic expression of human fulfillment: In the liturgy, the human being comes to him- or herself; each finds her or his own essential being."

Thus it can be said that the liturgy is an expressive action in two senses: It expresses, on the one hand, God's turning toward human beings for their salvation and, on the other hand, the praising, venerating, and petitioning response of human beings to God. The action of worship includes a self-fulfillment of the human person, but primarily it is an action of God, done for human persons through Christ in the Holy Spirit. The liturgy is an effective, saving, symbolic expression of both aspects.

This liturgical expression is dependent on the idea of what it means to be human and the image of the world that the particular society or culture has, as well as its image of God. Sequeira describes three forms of expression as basic dimensions both of general human actions and of those which are specifically religious and connected with worship. He distinguishes between verbal forms of expression ("These extend from simple words and phrases to artistic poetic texts, from the prayers of individuals to extended community prayers"); tonal expressions ("Especially singing, which unites not only word and tone, but also expressive movement, is one of the elementary forms of religious expression"); and expressive forms of motion ("Since every cult is action, it appears by its very nature as physical movement, is embodied in mimicry, gestures and postures, in steps, processions, dance, and in the most widely varying, often very complex sequences of action, including washing, anointing, sharing meals, etc.").

Liturgical action is thus at all times an expression of the Church's community life and exists in the tension between the unity of the whole Church and the multiplicity of the local Churches. For the sake of the inculturation of faith and liturgy, the liturgy constitution itself rejected "rigid uniformity" (*SC* 37). The liturgical books therefore anticipate a variety of choices and possibilities of adaptation so that celebrations may be suitable for the particular situation. As a result, the verbal and tonal forms of expression and those of movement can take a wide variety of shapes, and this does not contradict the substantial unity of the Church in essentials (cf. *SC* 38), for it expresses the catholicity of the Church, which in itself means unity in multiplicity.

So it can make a great deal of sense to speak of expressions instead of signs. The new Handbook of Liturgical Studies thus distinguishes between verbal and nonverbal forms of expression and includes spatial, sensual, and movement-related categories among the dimensions of liturgical expression.

ON THE SYMBOLIC CHARACTER
OF SACRAMENTS

18

Sacramental Formulae

In the first several centuries, the liturgy of the sacraments was understood as a celebration in which the community thanked and praised God for God's saving activity in order then to ask God once again to bring salvation to the community in this celebration. The faithful community was certain that God was really at work within it to bring it to salvation. It did not need any particular formulae for administering the sacraments: At baptism the one to be baptized made a confession of faith in the triune God and water was poured on him or her; when new ministers were consecrated hands were laid on them while a consecratory prayer of thanks and petition was spoken.

Then, in the early Middle Ages, the question of exactly when and how the sacrament happens began to come to the fore. It was always clear that there had to be an action and a word of explanation, either in prayer or in profession of faith. Augustine said of the blessing of the baptismal water: "The word is added to the element, and the sign of salvation [*sacramentum*] comes to be." But now the legalistic aspect became increasingly central, and as it did so, a narrowing of vision quite naturally followed. It was no longer the celebration as a whole that was interesting, but more and more what the Scholastics called "matter" and "form": The matter in the proper sense *(materia proxima)* is the central action; matter in the wider sense *(materia remota)* is the element. More precisely: The *materia proxima* in baptism is the pouring, while the *materia remota* is the water; in the Eucharist, the former is the meal, the latter the bread and wine. The "form" is the effective word which makes the material element a sacred sign; however, this was no longer seen to be the prayer of gratitude and petition but a formula of administration. In baptism, the confession of faith of the catechumen and the community was no longer sufficient; there had to be an indicative expression by the priest: "I baptize you. . . ."

Whereas in the beginning, then, the sacrament was shaped by a deprecative prayer, added to the action, which asked for God's gift, now this was reduced to an indicative formula of administration. This was the case at baptism and in the sacrament of penance. For the Eucharist a formula was also established, namely, a part of the Eucharistic prayer, which, in a true sense, is only exegetically and not liturgically called an account of institution; for these words, introduced by a relative clause, are neither a reading nor a formula but really the central part of the Eucharistic prayer of thanks and petition. Here, then, an indicative formula was not chosen, for if it were, the priest would have had to say: "Bread, I say to you: become the body of Christ." In contrast to the other sacraments, it was always maintained that these words alone were not sufficient for the consecration: The whole Eucharistic prayer had to be recited.

In celebrating the sacraments, however, one was always reminded above all to perform with painful exactitude that part of the rite that medieval theology had regarded as essential for the effectiveness of the sacrament—for example, the words of consecration, the formula of baptism, etc.—while the remaining "ceremonies" were often gabbled through as rapidly as possible and were only done at all because they were prescribed, even though they were seen as inessential to the effectiveness of the sacrament. In this we were blind to the clarifying, didactic, and pedagogical functions of the liturgical signs and to their influence on the indispensable cooperation of the recipient, since his or her faith is co-decisive for the sacrament's effect.

When our understanding of the sacraments was so crippled and the estimation placed on their objective effectiveness was so one sided, it was unimportant whether the signs were understood or not. Pretenses were often produced in place of the signs (see ch. 15 above), and no value at all was placed on the comprehensibility of the words. In contrast, the Council says distinctly that the sacraments "not only presuppose faith, but by words and objects they also nourish, strengthen, and express it; that is why they are called 'sacraments of faith.' " (SC 59).

19

On the Forms of
Sacramental Liturgies

In the renewal of the sacramental liturgies, an effort has been made to emphasize and revalue all the signs that clarify the event taking place. In contrast to preconciliar thinking, for which the minimum necessary for the validity of a sacrament was sufficient—that is, matter and form, a sign and the formula of administration associated with it—we now read of "principal elements" of the sacraments, which should be clearly evident in their celebration. Only in case of necessity will it still be sufficient—for example, at baptism—to pour water over the one to be baptized and say "I baptize you in the name of the Father and of the Son and of the Holy Spirit." In other words, what we have long referred to as "matter" and "form" are only part of the principal elements in a normal celebration of a sacrament. For marriage, the following principal elements are listed: the service of the Word, with proclamation of the Word of God; the exchange of promises, with the solemn blessing of the bride and groom (see ch. 27 below); the celebration of the Eucharist, with reception of the Eucharistic gifts; and, as "high point," the affirmation of their marriage by the couple.

In the different sacraments an attempt has been made, in various ways, to unite what is regarded as the legal formula of administration more closely with the other essential symbols within the liturgical celebration. The anamnetic-epicletic element is always central: The prayer, in the Holy Spirit, of thanks, praise, and petition for God's saving action. In this prayer, which is a part of every sacramental celebration, the sign of the word explains what it is that the community asks of God in this concrete celebration.

The ordination of priests offers an especially clear example of the alteration undergone in the meaning of the signs. For centuries, the giving of the paten and chalice was seen as the essential sign, and the words spoken were regarded as the formula of the sacrament. This now reads: "Accept from the holy people of God the gifts to be offered to him. Know what you are doing, and imitate the mystery you celebrate: Model your life on the mystery of the Lord's cross." These words, which used to be regarded as decisive for the reception of the sacrament of orders, are now only part of the explanatory rites. The core of the ordination is seen to be the imposition of hands by the bishop and the prayer of ordination which he then speaks—an anamnetic-epicletic prayer. Within this prayer are the sentences which, while they have a special importance as part of the prayer, can nevertheless no longer be described by the technical term "formula": "Grant to this servant of yours the dignity of the priesthood. Renew within him the Spirit of holiness. As a co-worker with the order of bishops may he be faithful to the ministry that he receives from you, Lord God, and be to others a model of right conduct."

In baptism, the older indicative form, "I baptize you . . ." was retained, but now the "praise and invocation of God over the water" is a central element of the celebration—the anamnetic-epicletic prayer of consecration, which gives a theological exposition of what happens in baptism (see ch. 21 below). And the threefold confession of faith in Father, Son, and Holy Spirit is also among the most important elements.

The consecratory prayer in the sacrament of anointing of the sick is the prayer over the oil (see ch. 26 below). If oil that has already been consecrated by the bishop is used, there should be a prayer of thanks that preserves the anamnetic-epicletic character. Here also, the anointing of forehead and hands is accompanied by explanatory words, which, however, are connected to the other signs in the celebration.

In the celebration of reconciliation, as in baptism, the indicative formula has been retained: "I absolve you . . .", but it follows a reading from Scripture, confession, and acceptance of penance, as well as a prayer by the penitent—elements meant to underscore the fact that reconciliation is also a liturgical celebration—and is embedded in the following anamnetic-epicletic prayer spoken while the priest rests his hand on the head of the penitent:

> God, the Father of mercies, through the death and resurrection of his Son has reconciled the world to himself and sent the Holy Spirit among us for the forgiveness of sins; through the ministry of the Church may God give you pardon and peace, and I absolve you from your sins in the name of the Father, and of the Son, and of the Holy Spirit. Amen.

Here the structure of the prayer is clear: a statement about the reconciling, saving action of God for the world through Christ in the Holy Spirit, and a request for this gift of God for this particular penitent, here and now.

In confirmation, the bishop says, while making the sign of the cross with chrism on the forehead of the confirmand: "Be sealed with the gift of the Holy Spirit." Immediately before this he opens his arms while praying the anamnetic-epicletic prayer in which, addressing God the Father, he acknowledges that these Christians have already received baptism. In the same prayer he then asks that the Holy Spirit be sent.

So in every case the words that were formerly known by the technical name, "formula of administration," are now in some way directed toward or united with a prayer of thankfulness and petition. This prayer clarifies, through the sign of the word, what is meant by the symbolic action belonging to it. Thus, while it is true that the explanatory words belonging to each sacrament have been retained, they are always expanded through the deprecatory element, the petition for God's saving action.

20

The Symbolic Character
of Baptism

Baptism, like all liturgy, is an event that takes place under the form of signs that, by their very nature, are meant to be understood and consciously carried through in the same action. Here again we find that in the past the signs were much distorted and made into codes or imitations (as, for example, when in place of the baptismal garment, a handkerchief was laid over the person being baptized!). Consequently, for baptism as for the other sacraments, the liturgical texts and actions have been reshaped in such a way that the visible and audible signs can be more easily understood.

It is necessary to keep in mind that the signs can only be understood within the context of the communicative action in which each of them is used. Communicative actions are those events which are typical for a certain group—and thus for the Christian community also—in which the group expresses and discovers its very nature. It is an advantage of more recent sacramental theology, particularly as regards liturgical actions and the way they are understood, that sacramental celebrations are understood as a particular kind of communicative action. From that point of view, for example, it is not sufficient for an understanding of the significance of the water of baptism simply to refer to its secular or profane meaning, even though that may be an important precondition of a proper understanding.

> Water does not have, in and of itself, any particular symbolic character. It can become a symbol. It has a fundamental appropriateness for that purpose, because and in so far as it appears in various forms of

human communication and has its place there: as a life-threatening element, as something which attracts, as a refreshing drink and a bath that refreshes and renews. . . . The sacraments cannot be unlocked simply on the basis of an elementary or "natural" symbolism. This "natural" symbolism corresponds, in a considerable degree, to an earlier context of life in which water had this kind of eloquence of meaning. In a technical approach to life, this context has changed, and with it, what water "says" to people in everyday life. But if, on the contrary, baptism is explained from the point of view of the reality to which it corresponds, if this reality is the central subject of pre-baptismal catechesis and of the celebration itself, then the use of water will begin to speak for itself (Peter Hünermann).

We can see this especially in the Easter Vigil celebration. The readings before the blessing of the baptismal water recall the beginnings of creation, the original chaos, the passage to freedom through the water; all of this expresses in truly elementary fashion the new life in whose context the use of baptismal water becomes a sign of divine action.

Thus an explanation of the baptismal liturgy can no longer be content simply to point to the pouring of water over the head of the one being baptized and the pronouncing of a formula of words. That would be merely a dogmatic-juridical way of speaking that restricts itself to what we formerly referred to, in a narrow understanding of liturgy, as "matter" and "form." It is no accident that the liturgical books have stopped using that expression, and speak instead of the main or essential elements of the liturgical celebration (see ch. 18 above). These include the Scripture readings of the Liturgy of the Word, but even more importantly the central, anamnetic-epicletic prayer (see ch. 19 above): In the case of baptism, this is the blessing of the baptismal water which, more than anything, reveals the meaning of the water as a symbol of baptism (see ch. 21 below).

It is an essential aim of the renewal to make the sacraments once again signs of the community of Christians with their Lord Jesus Christ and with one another. In them, and therefore in the celebration of baptism as well, the action of the whole Church as actualization of the priestly activity of Christ is accomplished in a twofold aspect: the gift of salvation and the praise of God. The dialogical structure of all liturgical action, from God to human persons and from humanity to God, is realized in its saving-descending aspect and in its ascending aspect in the whole liturgical celebration. The earlier distinction between divine worship (cult) and sacrament (saving gift) has been finally and completely overcome in the new order of things. The liturgical celebration of baptism, therefore, in each of its elements, is both testimony of salvation and praise of God: It is a structure of communicative action in which, though we can distinguish between the more important parts and those rites which serve primarily to interpret the action, we cannot dispense with important symbols—including the word—without suffering a severe loss.

21

"Praising and Invoking God over the Water" as Principal Element of Baptism

The water for baptism is no longer blessed only at the Easter Vigil, as used to be the case. Now, except during the fifty days of Easter, it is blessed at each celebration of baptism. What is the meaning of this sign? For the water is not consecrated like the Eucharistic gifts: It is not changed as they are.

In the preliminary remarks to The Instruction for Celebrating the Baptism of Children, we find that "the celebration of the sacrament is immediately preceded by: (a) the solemn prayer of the celebrant, who, by invoking God and recalling his plan of salvation, blesses the water of baptism . . ." (18). "Praise of God and calling God upon the water" thus immediately precede the renunciation of Satan, confession of faith, and the baptism itself as central elements of every baptism. In *The Rite for Christian Initiation of Adults* the theological import of this prayer of blessing is described in this way:

> [it recalls] the wonderful works of God from the creation of the world and the human race to the mystery of God's love; then by calling on the Holy Spirit and by the announcing of the death and rising of Christ, the newness of the washing of regeneration by the Lord is taught; through baptism we share in his death and rising and are made the holy people of God (210).

This clearly expresses the importance of this prayer for the whole baptismal celebration. Its structure, for which we have a choice of four

71

formulae, corresponds to that of all consecratory and blessing prayers (see ch. 19 above). It is determined by the elements of anamnesis (remembrance of God's saving deeds) and epiclesis (petition for the Holy Spirit to continue the divine work of salvation in the community). The first formula contains the following sequence of ideas: God is praised for God's saving work under the symbol of water; creation, the Flood, and Israel's passage through the Red Sea are mentioned, together with Jesus' baptism, the piercing of his side from which blood and water flowed out, and the command to the disciples to baptize. All this makes up the anamnetic part of the prayer. The epiclesis follows, asking the Father to send the Holy Spirit so that those who are baptized in Jesus Christ will attain to eternal life with him.

> Since God has always been revealed as the God who rescues, who makes all things good, ultimately in the Pasch of the Messiah, the Church calls on God, praying that God will again show Godself in power now, in the symbol of water, by bringing salvation to these persons who are to be baptized. The epicletic word is underscored by an epicletic gesture: the dipping of the Easter candle in the water, touching the water with the hand, or making a sign of the cross over the water (B. Kleinheyer).

Thus this rite is not intended to be a blessing of the water: It points toward the use to be made of this water, baptism itself. This central symbol creates a union between the one baptizing and the one being baptized as well as with all those present. It clarifies, through symbolic language, what is now happening to the one asking for baptism. We are confident in faith, as demonstrated by our prayer, that God, through this action of ours, will make present and effective, for the sake of the one being baptized, all of God's saving actions past and future. The invitation to prayer, which introduces the acclamation of praise, emphatically explains all this when it calls on all those present: "Let us ask God, the almighty Father, to bless this font, that those reborn in it may be made one with his adopted children in Christ." This element of adoption into the one people of God is regarded as so important that even in cases of baptism in danger of death (emergency baptism), it is to be included at the conclusion of the petitions.

The prescription that in the Easter season, until Pentecost, the water blessed during the Easter Vigil is to be used for baptism "in order better to express the close connection between baptism and the paschal mystery" is not very persuasive. Even then there is, of course, a prayer of praise, but without a petition for blessing. It is certainly correct, theologically speaking, to witness to the unity of the Easter celebration throughout the whole Easter season. But it is not at all clear why the blessing of the water should not be done during that time, precisely because, in that season, emphasis should be laid on the relationship between baptism and the paschal mystery.

22

Symbol of Living Water: The Baptismal Font

If the baptismal water is to be blessed at every baptismal liturgy except in the Easter season, the baptismal font will remain empty most of the time. What good is a font if it is apparently superfluous in the new baptismal liturgy? The prefatory remarks in the German edition of *The Rite for the Baptism of Children* have apparently anticipated this question, and prescribe: "In any case, the pastor should take care that the baptismal font is retained in the church. It should be the place of baptism and, when possible, should be the receptacle in which the water is blessed. Even at those times when it does not contain baptismal water, it serves to remind the faithful of their own baptism" (51).

The following criteria were always prescribed for the construction of the font: It should have a special place in the church building; its location should be appropriate for baptisms; it should be the real locus of baptism.

All these criteria still hold for the font within the renewed liturgy. If we take this as our starting point, we can deduce some further indications of how it should be constructed and placed. The communal celebration demanded by the nature of baptism, if possible in connection with a community Eucharist on Sunday, demands that the place for baptism be visible to the assembly. Thus, special baptismal chapels or fonts located at the entrance of the church are practically out of the question; instead, the font should be placed near the altar—although, at the same time, a crowding together of functional loci in the sanctuary ought to be avoided. In any case, it must at least be possible for all those participating in the baptism to gather around the font.

23

The Sunday Memorial of Baptism

Faith requires symbols of memory and intensification. Such a symbol, for the recollection of baptism, is the Sunday baptismal ritual. The new Missal says: "On Sundays, the baptismal ritual (sprinkling with holy water) may replace the general rite of penance." This is a custom whose roots reach far back into the first millennium. At first it took place in religious houses where, on Sunday mornings, there was a procession during which the rooms of the cloister and the church were sprinkled with holy water, and afterward the people present were also sprinkled. Since the high Middle Ages this rite has been employed as a memorial of baptism: The community confesses its faults before God, begs God's mercy, and is sprinkled with blessed water. This denotes a penitential spirit, a preparation for the Eucharistic celebration, and a remembrance of baptism; for as baptism wipes out all guilt, so also this sprinkling should remind us of our failings in the week just past and be for us a sign of conversion.

It is gratifying that this old *Asperges* procession, including the blessing of the water and its sprinkling, has been revived as a memorial of our own baptism, for baptism *is* conversion and renewal of life *(metanoia)*. When this rite is used, of course, the normal acknowledgment of sin at the beginning of Mass must be omitted, since it would be a duplication. In addition, through the sign of sprinkling, the opening rites, which too often seem stiff and wordy, acquire a more lively and celebratory character. This ritual sign can be performed at all the Sunday Masses, including the one on Saturday evening. On special feasts, such as that of the Baptism of the Lord or Pentecost, it could be given a distinctive character. The blessing of the water should be done in the presence of the community. The baptismal font or area is especially suitable, if it is visible to the community (see ch. 22 above). The Easter candle should be prominent. In all this, the movement to the place of baptism and the sprinkling with water must be adapted to modern sensibilities so that these can be a symbol in the fullest sense, a memorial and renewal of baptism.

After an invitation to prayer and a short period of silence, a blessing is spoken over the water, recalling God's saving deeds done through water for God's people and asking for the extension of God's work of salvation here and now. The sprinkling can be done from the altar or during a procession through the church while the community sings an appropriate song, for example, on the theme of baptism, resurrection, or repentance and conversion. It is a good idea to use the same hymns or antiphons often in this rite so that they produce a kind of signal effect in the assembly. After the song is over, when the priest returns to the altar, the rite should close with a prayer: "May almighty God cleanse us of our sins, and through the Eucharist we celebrate make us worthy to sit at his table in his heavenly kingdom." Between the blessing of the water and the congregation's song there can also be a blessing of salt, if salt is to be put into the water. Salt is a symbol of strength. Therefore salt is blessed in order that "wherever this salt and water are sprinkled," God may "drive away the power of evil, and protect us always by the presence of his Holy Spirit."

Every Sunday is a little Easter, the celebration of the weekly Pasch. What could be more appropriate than to recall, from time to time in this Easter feast, the connection between Eucharist and baptism: "Renew the living spring of your life within us and protect us in spirit and body" (from the prayer of blessing over the water).

24

Baptismal Anointings: Interpretive Symbols

Two anointings are prescribed for every baptism: one with the oil of catechumens after the petitions and prayer of exorcism, immediately before the blessing of the baptismal water and so just preceding the core of the baptismal ritual; the second with chrism (a mixture of oil and perfumes, especially balsam), immediately after baptism (see ch. 38 below). The anointing with chrism is especially important, for it points to the royal priesthood of the baptized and their membership in the Anointed One, the Christ. At the same time it is connected with the sacrament of confirmation, in which the baptized are again anointed with chrism. For that reason this anointing is omitted after baptism if those baptized are to be confirmed in the same ceremony, something which is permitted for the baptism of any adult, even by a priest (and especially at the Easter Vigil). If only baptism is being administered, the anointing with chrism may not be omitted (except when baptism is given to one in danger of death). Although, like the anointing with the oil of catechumens just before the center of the baptismal ritual, it is one of the interpretive rituals, it presents us, in symbolic form, with some extremely important statements of faith. Christ is the One anointed with chrism, the Messiah; thus this anointing is a symbol of the most precious gift of God, the Holy Spirit, for the one baptized belongs now—according to the text of the accompanying prayer—"for ever to Christ, who is anointed eternally as priest, king, and prophet." So the anointing with chrism calls our attention to our incorporation in the ecclesial community in its fullest form: Believers become Christians through the baptismal bath, through anointing at confirmation, and through participation in the Eucharistic feast. There are thus three steps: washing, anointing, and meal, quite in line with ordinary procedure in secular life in ancient times.

In contrast, the anointing with the oil of catechumens is optional and is very often omitted. There are at least two reasons for this: First of all, without an adequate catechesis it is scarcely comprehensible that there should be two anointings; secondly, this anointing does not have any content that goes beyond the preceding prayer of exorcism, in which we have asked that the one being baptized be protected from the Evil One. This is clear from the prayer attached to the anointing: "We anoint you with the oil of salvation in the name of Christ our Savior. May he strengthen you with his power, who lives and reigns for ever and ever." So the anointing with the oil of catechumens is meant to call down the power of the Lord, while the anointing with chrism shows that the one baptized receives a share in the royal and prophetic priesthood of the Lord.

25

First Communion
and the Baptismal Candle

We can see from a mother's letter how little comprehension of symbolic forms of expression there often is, even in those who are responsible for planning and carrying out liturgical services:

> When I made my First Communion in 1960, the renewal of baptismal promises and the use of the baptismal candle were still important parts of the celebration. But this year, when my son received his First Communion, it was explained to us that since the Second Vatican Council the baptismal promises had been eliminated, and therefore the use of the baptismal candle at Communion no longer made any sense. I regret that very much, because it surely does make sense to emphasize the relationship between baptism and Eucharist, especially at the celebration of First Communion.

The mother goes on to ask whether this "new order of things" might not simply be a permissive decree. She simply cannot believe that symbols which seem meaningful to her would be "eliminated." And she is quite right! If they treat the symbolic usages in the liturgy in such fashion, and this in the name of liturgical reform, what must the liturgical services of this community as a whole look like?

Certainly, there are no precise directions for the shape of First Communion celebrations, nor have there ever been any. In that sense, there was nothing that could really be "eliminated." We are not talking about a children's Mass here, but of a parish worship service in which children are permitted for the first time to share fully in the Eucharistic meal, thus taking a further step forward in their integration in the community and in the Christian life. The *Werkbuch zum*

Gotteslob (Workbook for the Catholic Common Prayer Book) vol. 7, describes this quite correctly:

> The first reception of Holy Communion is a continuation of the way begun at baptism, the crown of Christian initiation. Its connection with holy baptism is made visible in the white garment and the burning candle, which is really the baptismal candle: The children thus, in a manner of speaking, move visibly from the font to the altar.

Obviously there cannot be a liturgical form that is the same for all communities or parishes because the circumstances differ so widely: the age of the children and the form of their initiation, whether in school classes or in Communion groups, as well as the time of year, for it is not the custom everywhere, as it is in Germany, to hold First Communions on the Sunday after Easter. Or consider the possible combination of baptism, First Communion, and confirmation in a single celebration, which is given as a possibility in the liturgical book on the initiation of school-age children into the Church.

But clearly, the baptismal candle ought to have a special place in the celebration. For practical reasons, the children usually no longer hold them in their hands; they place them around the altar. It makes good sense to have the candles solemnly lit from the Easter candle, even outside of the Easter season. In one parish, the candles are taken from the altar after Communion and given back to the children, with the following words:

> Once your baptismal candle was lit from the Easter candle; now your Communion candle has also been lit from the Easter candle. It is a sign that Christ is not only among us under the form of bread, but lives with us when we are kind to one another and bring one another light and joy. Take your candles, and bear the light of Christ into your families, into our community, and to everyone you meet.

This mother's letter shows that for her, the connection between the sacraments of initiation into the Church, that is, the union of baptism and Eucharist, was vividly present in the symbol of the baptismal candle. It appears that such a symbol remains much more clearly in our memory than do Communion instruction classes, no matter how well prepared, if the latter only convey intellectual knowledge. The letter turns a veritable spotlight on the real importance that symbols have in the lives of the faithful.

26

Symbols of Healing
in Sickness

It is clearly evident in the new order for the anointing of the sick that, in the celebration of the sacraments, not only should individual symbols be taken up and explicated in and for themselves, but the whole progress of the celebration unites the most varied symbols in such a way that, in a certain sense, a single, common symbol comes into existence (see ch. 14 above). There is scarcely another sacrament that is so burdened by a one-sided historical development in its praxis. Even the change of the name from "last anointing" to "anointing of the sick" in the *Common Catechism* of 1955 apparently had little effect. The old habit, whereby the priest was only called when there was no longer any hope for the continuance of earthly life, was too ingrained. Since then we have, in the English-speaking countries, *Pastoral Care of the Sick: Rites of Anointing and Viaticum*. In this book the accent is again clearly placed where it lay in the earliest centuries: on assistance aimed at healing the sick and not primarily on those who are evidently about to die. The German-speaking bishops already realized that they had to exert themselves if they hoped to achieve their goal by changing the entrenched mentality. Thus in their introductory remarks they express the hope that "through a renewed proclamation and through the enthusiasm of those who exercise pastoral care" there may be "a decisive change in sacramental praxis," to be compared to the change from rare to more frequent reception of Communion, so that

> it will be regarded as equally normal that the earlier—often feared—
> "last anointing" will become in the future the comforting "celebra-

tion of the anointing of the sick" and that it will be welcomed by the sick as their own sacrament, one that is part of the everyday life of a Christian community, a hospital, or a home for the aged.

The bishops even call for "a new faith-consciousness and a new public opinion in the Church."

It must be one of the aims of pastoral care of the sick to see to it that anointing again becomes the sacrament of the sick in our communities. Its place in our lives is not the point at which we see the end approaching, and thus it should not be seen simply as death's precursor. It is an encounter with Christ, who wants to lift up the sick person in his or her oppressive situation, as the Letter of James says: "Are any among you sick? Let them call for the elders of the church, and let them pray over them, anointing them with oil in the name of the Lord; and the prayer of faith will save those who are sick, and the Lord will raise them up; and if they have committed sins, they will be forgiven" (Jas 5:14-15). There is not a word about death and dying in this scriptural passage! A careful exegesis of the Greek words for "save" and "raise up" shows clearly that what is intended is bodily and spiritual healing. Just as Jesus showed himself to be one who opposes and overcomes sickness (Matt 4:24: "they brought him all the sick, those afflicted with various diseases and pains, . . . and he healed them"), so the Christian community must follow his command (Matt 10:8: "heal the sick"). Scripture sees the healings as signs of the fact that in Jesus Christ, God has entered into dominion and the reign of God has begun. In the healing of the sick, God is self-revealed as the salvation of all humankind. And so it must be the deepest concern of Christian communities not to leave the sick alone but to stand by them so that they can become whole again and learn to endure their sickness in faith. The saving symbol of the anointing of the sick is, in a certain sense, the most compressed form of this concern for the sick. Thus we can say that the sacrament of the dying is not primarily the anointing of the sick, but viaticum, the reception of the Eucharist according to the Lord's word: "Those who eat my flesh and drink my blood have everlasting life, and I will raise them up at the last day" (John 6:54).

There are three steps in raising up the sick: visiting them, bringing them Communion, and anointing them. The sacrament is also a part of the whole complex of service given to the sick. Only afterward do we find in the liturgical book a chapter which, because sickness and death have a common root, is directly concerned with the dying. Anointing is not just consolation and promise of salvation for an individual; it is an event of divine worship in an evil and distorted situation which is the fate of all humanity and which is borne sympathetically by the whole community. In it the action of the whole Church is accomplished as actualization of the priestly work of Christ in its twofold aspect: the extension of salvation to humanity, and humanity's worship of God. The healing-descending aspect is expressed particularly in sacrament and proclamation of Scripture; the praising-ascending aspect in prayer, praise, and thanks to God. Both are closely combined in the anointing of the sick. Therefore it begins with a service of the Word in which God's promise of salvation is prominent. In the petitions, the blessing of the oils, and the prayer of faith after the anointing, the aspect of prayer ascending from us to God is expressed. In the new formula of words to accompany the anointing, the work of the Lord in saving and raising up the sick person through the Holy Spirit is accented. The forgiveness of sins is, in accordance with the scriptural evidence, a secondary consequence and so is expressed as a fact accompanying the main action. These words are addressed to the sick person, as are the gestures of anointing and imposition of hands.

The silent laying on of hands is one of the essential symbols in the rite. It forms the transition between the petitions at the close of the Liturgy of the Word and the anointing which follows. Those who are seriously ill, in particular, will experience this form of total attention and giving as an expression of sympathy and encouragement. The blessing of the oil or, if it has already been blessed by the bishop on Holy Thursday (see ch. 38 below), the prayer of thanksgiving over the oil gives a theological interpretation of what is taking place: It recalls God's saving deed through Christ for sick people and asks for a renewed bestowal of this saving and healing gift on this person who is ill. The prayer after the anointing is a renewed petition, an expression of trust and of faith in God's help. The anointing—for which any vegetable oil may be used—is no longer of the five senses, which used to be regarded as portals for attack and tools of sin. Instead, the oil is placed on the forehead and the hands. This sign, when done as it should be, ought to be quite understandable even today.

The anointing of the sick is thus, like all liturgy, an event and a deed done under sacred signs that from their very nature are meant to be understood and performed consciously and actively. There will certainly be a division of opinions about the symbolic character of the signs used in the anointing. But the intention of the renewal was to make the apostolic praxis once more clearly evident and to express the content of the sacrament itself in the signs that are employed. The way in which the symbols are carried out is one of the most important aspects. Haste and brevity must never be the keys; the manner in which the sacrament is administered should not give the impression that it is a routine affair.

27

The Marriage Blessing as Symbol of God's Promise of Salvation

Among the principal elements of the liturgical celebration of marriage, according to *The Rite of Marriage,* is "the special nuptial blessing for the bride and for the marriage covenant." It is therefore prescribed for every solemnization of marriage, whether within the Mass or outside it.

The various names for this blessing ("nuptial blessing" or "blessing of the newly married") indicate a certain amount of unclarity. The reasons lie especially in the history of the development of this blessing, which has not yet been fully explained. Christians in the first several centuries had no obligatory form for marriage; they simply adopted the customs of their various cultures, although of course they excised any obviously pagan rituals. The Jewish Christians would certainly have retained the marriage *beraka,* a prayer said after the legal formalities of the marriage, praising and thanking God for creation and asking God's assistance for the married couple. That is, in fact, the basic structure of Judeo-Christian prayer: thanking God for God's saving deeds in the past (anamnesis) and asking God for salvation and help in the future as well (epiclesis).

In the Eastern liturgies, this blessing was always said over both partners and was regarded as indispensably necessary for the sacrament. The Roman liturgy developed differently. It is true that here, too, there may originally have been a prayer for the couple. But at the beginning of the medieval period, the blessing and the bestowal of the

85

bridal veil were already connected, so that a parallel came to be drawn between the consecration of virgins and the blessing of a bride. Like the virgin given to Christ, her Bridegroom, the bride received a veil and a special blessing. It would be a question in itself as to what extent this development can be explained in light of the position of women in the Middle Ages. The woman was bound to her husband with a ring, the sign of her fidelity. In any case, the West retained only a blessing of the bride that in itself was of no importance for the marriage itself, which took place through the consent, the yes given and received by the two people. Only as a result of the conciliar reform of the liturgy did it become obligatory, as in the Eastern liturgies, to speak the "great prayer of blessing" over the partners. In German-speaking countries this follows immediately after the exchange of promises, the giving of the ring, and the affirmation of the marriage by the presider. However, it remains without legal import for the actual administration of the sacrament.

Here, however, it becomes increasingly important to ask about the relative value of liturgical actions and legal actions. In other sacraments, the solemn prayer of blessing or consecration is often constitutive—for example, the prayers of consecration at the ordination of deacons, priests, and bishops. If we disavow the idea that every union between baptized persons is automatically a sacrament (a point of view that does not give sufficient weight to the importance of faith as a necessary precondition for every sacrament), then, as in the East, the exchange of consent could be regarded as the necessary precondition for the sacrament of marriage, which is actually constituted by the marriage blessing.

But even without such a development there can be no doubt that the essential matter of faith is expressed in the prayer of blessing. Therefore we can no longer speak of a bridal blessing. This prayer is a solemn marriage blessing.

The liturgy for marriage also unites a bundle of individual symbols to form the one great symbol, God's promise of salvation, which is celebrated and asked of God in this sacrament. The prayer of blessing, spoken while the presider lays hands on the couple is, after the consent of the pair, the most important symbol in this liturgical celebration.

28

The Uplifted Bread, the Uplifted Cup

There really are two different elevations, a "little" and a "great" one. At the point in the narrative of institution when the priest says the words "He took bread and gave thanks," he takes the bread and lifts it a little above the altar. In saying the narrative of institution over the chalice, he likewise takes it and lifts it slightly. We have long forgotten the meaning of this sign, especially since it used to be done while the priest's back was turned to the congregation and so was invisible. This ancient "little" elevation of bread and chalice goes back to the paschal meal rituals which are still used by Jews today, in which the head of the household—and so, probably, Jesus at the Last Supper—lifts the bread and cup a little while speaking the words of blessing. It seems well established that this gesture is one of offering, since the paschal supper was, at the same time, a sacrificial meal.

The "great" elevation is something different. The Missal says: "He [the priest] shows the community the consecrated host; then he places it on the paten and genuflects." There is a similar instruction with regard to the chalice. This elevation first appears in the Middle Ages and is connected with the question that was debated at that time, namely: At exactly what point in the Eucharistic prayer did the change in the elements from bread and wine to Body and Blood of Christ take place? Around the year 1200, the weight of assent fell to the proposition that the change in the bread takes place immediately after the corresponding words of institution and before the words are spoken over the chalice. Thereafter the custom quickly arose for the priest to bend his knee in adoration immediately after speaking the words of institution over the bread and to repeat this gesture after the words over the chalice. But since he was celebrating with his back to the congregation their view of the species was obstructed, and the elevation, which was now becoming customary, represented a signal to the congregation also to look adoringly at the host. Instead of turning around and showing the host to the people, the priest lifted it high over his head.

The corresponding gesture of showing the chalice, however, did not become commonplace before the sixteenth century—a clear indication that this cannot be an essential element of the ritual. The elevation of the Eucharistic bread was a response to the general desire of people at that period to look at the host. Since reception of Communion had become uncommon due to exaggerated reverence, the desire to see the Body of the Lord became stronger and stronger, until the idea developed that there could be an "ocular communion," a grace-giving contact with Christ through this holy stare. So the priest had to hold up the host as long as possible, often so long that assistants had to support his arms lest he grow tired. In large churches the next step was to connect the Masses at the individual altars with one another in such a way that the faithful could move in procession from one elevation to another, from altar to altar, and in this way could receive a richer share in the fruits of the sacrifice of the Mass. This quantitative notion of grace, while never a matter of Church teaching, was deeply rooted in popular belief.

From this point of view the origins of the Feast of Corpus Christi are easily understood: In a sense it prolongs and expands this elevation of the transformed species. The view of the sacred host in the monstrance is a prolongation of what, in the Mass, is restricted to the consecration: the presentation of the Body of Christ for adoration. For many people today, according to the Viennese liturgist Johannes H. Emminghaus, this medieval piety may represent "an unworthy combination of a religious core and a popular spectacle." But it is certain that, with the renewal of frequent Communion, the "holy stare" after the consecration has lost its meaning. For the same reason, the ringing of the bell before the consecration and at the elevation of bread and chalice, while still permitted by the Missal (GIRM

109), is really superfluous if one has a proper understanding of the Eucharistic prayer as a whole. In contrast to the Latin Mass of days gone by, when the Eucharistic prayer is spoken aloud and in the vernacular the congregation knows exactly when the words of institution occur. For the "great" elevation it is sufficient for the priest to lift bread and chalice chest high, thus preventing from the outset any harmful reminders of the medieval misunderstanding of this gesture.

29

The Distribution of Communion as Symbol: The Eucharistic Bread

The development of the distribution of Communion shows that the form of this symbol is not arbitrary. In it the Eucharistic piety of a particular time and place finds its expression.

In the earliest Christian communities, the Eucharistic species were certainly received in the way that is customary at meals: In Hellenistic culture the people would have reclined at table with their upper bodies leaning on the left elbow and slightly elevated. Pictorial representations from about the year 500 show the contemporary ritual, in which the species were given to the recipients while standing. The Lectionary of Bernward of Hildesheim (d. 1022) is the first witness to reception of Communion while kneeling, an attitude that only slowly penetrated the West between the eleventh and sixteenth centuries.

In the Byzantine liturgy, the faithful still receive Communion while standing. The place for reception has changed in the course of time. In the early Middle Ages in Rome the priest still brought Communion to the people, while in Gaul the faithful advanced to the altar. In North Africa they stood before the gates of the sanctuary, which were often chest high.

In this early period, Communion was received in the hand as a matter of course. Cyril of Jerusalem (d. 387) describes it this way: "When you go forward . . . make your left hand a throne for the right, which is to receive the king, and cup your hand and receive the Body of Christ and say 'Amen.' " Before it was eaten, the Body of Christ was to be touched to the eyes. Afterward, the chalice was presented. Other witnesses show the open hands laid over one another in the form of a cross and also indicate that the senses were blessed by being touched with the Eucharistic species. Before receiving the Eucharist, the laity were to wash their hands, and there was a special font for this in the basilicas. Often the hand of the one distributing communion was kissed before the Eucharist was received. Increasing reverence and anxiety about misuse of the sacred species—such as taking the host away to be used for magical purposes in the Middle Ages, whereas in the early centuries it was simply a matter of course that the faithful would take the Eucharist with them and keep it for Communion at home—led to the practice of placing the host in the communicant's mouth. That was done with increasing frequency, but not before the ninth century. The transition from Communion in the hand to Communion in the mouth coincided with the changeover from leavened to unleavened bread. Beginning in the thirteenth century it was customary, here and there, to spread a cloth before the communicants, who now knelt at the altar. And in the sixteenth century this cloth was laid over a bench placed between the nave and the sanctuary. From the seventeenth century onward, this became the communion rail, which appeared nearly everywhere in place of the rood screen (see ch. 48 below).

Up to the fourth century, the congregation normally communicated at every Eucharistic celebration. In fact, they communicated more often, since the community Eucharist was generally restricted to Sundays. By taking the Eucharist with them, they were able to receive Communion at home, often even as a daily custom before taking any other food. But then the reception of Communion receded with surprising speed, probably conditioned especially by notions of sinfulness. We find John Chrysostom (d. 407) complaining about this in the East, and Ambrose (d. 397) in the West. From the ninth century it seems to have become customary to receive Communion only once a year, which the Lateran Council of 1215 then prescribed as a new minimum: the Easter Communion.

These are probably the most important stages in this development, which shows that the changes introduced with Vatican Council II, once again making Communion in the hand an option, are an attempt to recover part of the original tradition of the first Christian centuries.

30

Breaking Bread:
The Misinterpretation of a Symbol

Occasionally (perhaps even increasingly?) we notice that priests, while saying "He took bread, blessed it, broke it, gave it to his disciples and said. . ." in the Eucharistic prayer, break the priest's host into several pieces. The new order of celebration, for very good reasons, prescribes this action only after the sign of peace, during the singing of the *Agnus Dei*. Even though breaking the bread while saying the corresponding words may seem appropriate at first glance, it obscures the real meaning of the fraction. From the beginning, the breaking of the bread has been the most important action preparatory to the distribution of the Eucharist. The symbolism already attached to this gesture in Judaism is essential: Through eating the one bread, broken into pieces and distributed to all, the table fellowship comes into existence (cf. 1 Cor 10:16-17). In this way, it is a sharing in the Body of Christ (cf. 1 Cor 5:7).

For this reason it is desirable that "the Eucharistic bread should be made in such a way that in a Mass with a congregation the priest is able actually to break the host into parts and distribute them to at least some of the faithful" (GIRM 283). And anyone who has been present when several large hosts are broken to be shared by all those participating in a Eucharistic gathering will certainly have found this to be much more meaningful than having a single host broken while the corresponding words are spoken in the Eucharistic prayer. It therefore becomes clear why the early Church referred to the whole event as "the breaking of the bread." And that is precisely the symbolic quality that we need to recover!

There is another consideration: If everything that is described in the words of the Eucharistic prayer were to be carried out immediately in symbolic action, the distribution would have to be done right after the words of institution, including both the eating of the bread and the drinking from the cup. It is more sensible to stick with the given order: taking bread and wine, prayer of thanks and praise, the Our Father as table prayer, breaking, and distribution.

31

The Symbol of the Eucharistic Cup

During most of the first millennium it was a matter of course to receive Communion under both forms: bread and wine. Pope Gelasius I (d. 496) sharply rejected the attitude of those who did not receive from the cup: "They should either receive the sacrament in its entirety or be kept from it altogether, since it is impossible to separate one and the same mystery without severe sacrilege." Only in cases of necessity could the cup be omitted; it was the usual thing even for Communion of infants, the sick, or travelers.

Anxiety about the possibility of spilling, however, led rather early to a change in the form of Communion from the cup in both East and West. One step may be seen in the practice of mixing, in the chalice prepared for distribution, only a few drops of consecrated wine with a quantity of unconsecrated wine and thus in a sense to minimize the danger of desecration. Another solution was to sanctify unconsecrated wine by dipping the host into it. In early medieval Rome, then, the people were no longer permitted to drink directly from the cup; they used drinking tubes. Outside Rome and in the Byzantine rite until the present time, the danger of spilling was avoided by placing the host in the consecrated wine and then giving it to the communicant. This was rejected in the West, mainly on the grounds that this was no longer an act of drinking. But this rejection, for the sake of preserving the original form of Communion from the cup, had the further consequence that, unlike in the East, the participation of the people in the cup was entirely abandoned. This development was carried to its completion in the twelfth and thirteenth centuries. There is no evidence that hygienic considerations played any role. It was probably, in the first instance, a matter of increasing reverence, the same feeling which, since the ninth century, had led to the change from leavened to unleavened bread and from Communion in the hand to Communion on the tongue. Also the desire to see the host, articulated in the elevation of the Eucharistic species after the consecration and later in Eucharistic processions, caused the chalice, whose contents were invisible, to be strongly de-emphasized. The dogmatic clarification which determined that the Body of Christ is entirely present even under the single species also contributed to this development.

It can hardly be surprising that the abandonment, and then even the forbidding of Communion in the cup for the laity, quickly led to serious clashes of opinion, culminating in the Reformation. And it is also worth noting—without in any way denying the truth of the theological statement that the Lord is present in even one species—that, as a result of the removal of the cup, Eucharistic piety was materially altered. Let me mention just two items: The community character of the Eucharist, which had been so clearly symbolized in the common cup and the covenant motif it represented, fell into the background; and it was no accident that the community symbolism of the breaking of bread was abandoned in favor of precut, small hosts. Both of these point in the direction of an individualizing of Communion piety. The withdrawal of the chalice made possible the separation of Communion from the celebration of the Eucharist, since the reserved hosts were now, with increasing frequency, received outside of Mass, and this was justified on the basis of greater recollection and devo-tion. This emigration of Communion from the Mass was a further step toward individualization and privatization of Eucharistic devotion. That these tendencies have not been fully overcome in our communities, despite the conciliar initiatives, is evident in the practice of giving Communion from the tabernacle and the continued rarity of the distribution of Communion under the form of wine. In addition, the previous isolation and exaltation of the celebrating priest were one set of consequences of forbidding the chalice to laypeople.

All this may make clear why the retrieval of the ancient Christian practice of Communion under both kinds is so important today and is not simply a liturgists' hobbyhorse (on this subject, see H. Spaemann, ed., ". . . *und trinket alle daraus." Zur Kelchkommunion in unseren Gemeinden* (Freiburg i. Br., 1986).

32

Obscuring the Symbolic Character of the Lord's Supper: When Communion Is Given from the Tabernacle

I was present at a Eucharist in a cathedral where Communion was not given from hosts consecrated at the celebration itself, but instead others were brought from the tabernacle; for this purpose, even before the recitation of the Our Father, candles were lighted on the altar holding the tabernacle, which stood in full view of those present, and the ciborium was solemnly borne to the altar of celebration. It is not uncommon in other churches as well to see distribution of Communion from the tabernacle (see ch. 50 below).

It really should no longer be possible for such a thing to happen in a bishop's church. For in fact, "all should hold in very high esteem the liturgical life of the diocese which centers around the bishop, especially in his cathedral church" (*SC* 41). The Council treated this very question: "Hearty endorsement is given to that closer form of participation in the Mass whereby the faithful, after the priest's Communion, receive the Lord's Body under elements consecrated at that very sacrifice" (*SC* 55). Incidentally, this goes back to decrees of Popes Benedict XIV and Pius XII. The practice in the Roman liturgy of distributing previously consecrated hosts is unknown in the Eastern Churches as well as in Protestantism, and it was practically absent in the West before the seventeenth century. The liturgist Emil J. Lengeling wrote as early as 1965 that "only an age that had no sense of genuine symbolism and concentrated narrowly on that which was regarded as 'essential' in the dogmatic sense could have been seduced into preferring the more convenient way to that which was better and more appropriate." And he adds a wish that, unfortunately, has not yet been fully accomplished: "We may well hope, after this emphatic challenge of the Council to us to do the sensible thing, that something that is offensive to non-Catholic Christians and that, nowadays, even alienates many Catholics will recede farther and farther into the past."

Postconciliar documents also bring the matter to our attention again and again. *The Eucharistic Instruction* of 1967 requires it: "Steps should be taken" and gives as a reason "in order that the Communion may stand out more clearly even through signs as a participation in the sacrifice actually being celebrated" (art. 31). And The General Instruction of the Roman Missal indicates that it is desirable "that the faithful receive the Lord's Body from hosts consecrated at the same Mass" (56h).

The English translation of the *Eucharistic Instruction* is, significantly enough, rather a softening of the Latin text, which would be better rendered "it is much to be desired." Consistently with this, the introduction to *Holy Communion and Worship of the Eucharist Outside Mass* 1976 (13) says:

> Sacramental Communion received during Mass is the more perfect participation in the Eucharistic celebration. The Eucharistic sign is expressed more clearly when the faithful receive the Body of the Lord from the same sacrifice after the Communion of the priest. Therefore, recently baked bread, for the Communion of the faithful, should ordinarily be consecrated in every eucharistic celebration.

The tabernacle is thus clearly to be used for distribution of Communion at Mass only in exceptional situations, for in the tabernacle "the principal reason for reserving the sacrament after Mass is to unite, through sacramental Communion, the faithful unable to participate in the Mass, especially the sick and the aged, with Christ and the offering of his sacrifice" (decree of the Congregation for the Sacraments, June 21, 1973).

Certainly, it is always the same Body of the Lord that is received.

But the symbolic character of the celebration of the Lord's Supper, which Christ gave us at the Last Supper with the command to "do this in memory of me," is obscured if the Eucharistic bread does not issue from the celebration in which those communicating are participants. No one should be complaining about a loss of symbolism in Catholic liturgy when, at the same time, the very symbols given us by the Lord himself are being treated in such cavalier fashion.

33

Symbols of Penance and Reconciliation

Since the bodily, visible dimension is part of being human, penance must also be expressed in visible signs and actions that reveal both the penitent's turning away from sin and his or her reintegration in the company of Christ's disciples and thus in faith, hope, and love. In addition to the works of penance known in the Old Testament (prayer, fasting, and almsgiving), which correspond to the concepts of piety, overcoming of self, and loving service, and which were always highly regarded in Christian communities, we could also think in modern terms: renunciation of certain forms of consumption, willingness to come to the aid of others (including what the Middle Ages called "the seven corporal works of mercy"), listening to the Word of God, meditation, and penitential liturgies. We need in all this to exclude any misunderstanding about justification by works, since every human act of penance is always anticipated by the grace of a loving God: It is only this which makes us capable of penance in the first place.

Out of concern for the reconciliation of sinners, the Church at various times and in different regions developed a variety of penitential practices of differing severity. Even the first communities knew of excommunication, the exclusion of sinners for a period of time in order to bring them to repentance (cf. 1 Cor 5:1-3). Prayer, fasting, and almsgiving as well as other good works were regarded as sufficient for the forgiveness of daily faults. The so-called deadly sins (especially apostasy, murder, and adultery) were, at a very early stage, subjected to public penance, which essentially consisted of the following steps: private confession in the presence of the bishop, reception into the status of penitent with assignment of particular penitential duties, exclusion from the Eucharistic celebration and from reception of Communion. The period of penance could last for years, in many places until one's deathbed. Reconciliation, the reception back into the community, was accomplished by an imposition of the bishop's hands. Beginning in the sixth century under the influence of peripatetic Irish and Scottish monks, the practice of so-called tariff penance was introduced: The penitent confessed his or her sins to a priest who assigned an appropriate penance; after it was completed (or, at a later period, immediately) the penitent received absolution. From this developed the custom of private confession, in which the ecclesial aspect scarcely played any further part. In the modern era the practice of devotional confession arose, with confession of only minor sins, especially as a preparation for Communion. From the sixteenth century onward the celebration of penance was moved from the sanctuary to the confessional. Even before this the priest's prayer that the sinner be forgiven had been replaced by the judicial formula, I absolve you . . .").

The liturgy of the early Church offered the faithful, who were conscious of the ongoing danger to their salvation (cf. 1 Cor 10:12; 2 Cor 4:7; Phil 2:12), special helps toward penitential attitudes and activities: the forty-day Lenten penitential period as a preparation for Easter, the cross of ashes on Ash Wednesday, the penitential rite in the Mass, penitential worship services as well as exhortations to repentance, and prayers for the penitents. Friday, the day of Christ's death, was a day for penance, on which in earlier times abstinence from meat was required as a penitential practice. Today we are asked to choose personal works of penance to be performed on that day.

The postconciliar reform of the penitential liturgy is intended to renew the sacrament in such a way that the symbols and texts used will more clearly express the nature and effect of this sacrament. Since 1975 there has been a study-text on the celebration of penance available. It contains the celebration of reconciliation for individuals in the confessional, including the elements of greeting, Scripture reading, confession and counsel, imposition of a penance, act of contrition, absolution, praise of God, and dismissal. Another form is given for community celebrations of reconciliation with individual confession and absolution, in which the confession and absolution are embedded in a service of the Word that emphasizes the liturgical-ecclesial character of penance. At communal celebrations of reconciliation with general confession and absolution (not permitted in German dioceses), individual confession is replaced by common acknowledgment of sins, and absolution is given to the whole congregation. Absolution is always accompanied by extension of the hands and a sign of the cross in order to indicate the connection between Jesus' death on the cross and the reconciliation of the penitent.

Nonsacramental penitential services bring to our consciousness aspects of the sacrament that had become distorted in the way the sacrament was administered heretofore. They are meant to sharpen consciences through intensive encounter with God's Word and common examination of conscience. On the model of liturgical services of the Word, they are made up of proclamation, reflection, and prayer.

The new order of the liturgy for penance and reconciliation, by developing the symbolic character of the sacrament, gives emphasis to two aspects in particular. First of all, it should be made evident that repentance and reconciliation do not involve merely an action that takes place between God and individual sinners, mediated by the priest, but that it is an event that affects the whole Christian community. Secondly, it is evident that there exists a variety of forms and symbolic actions of reconciliation in addition to the sacrament of reconciliation itself, which either complement the sacrament or lead us toward it.

34

Do Indulgences
Still Mean Anything?

Quite a few Catholics are asking today whether indulgences can still be appropriate contemporary signs of penance and reconciliation. If we distinguish between sacraments and sacramentals (see ch. 2 above), it is obvious that indulgences are not part of the central liturgical celebration of the sacraments and, at least in our country, they do not play a very prominent part in sacramental life as a whole. In fact, we might ask whether there is anything positive that can be said about the meaning and intention of the practice of granting indulgences.

In Germany, the best known of these is probably the so-called *portiuncula* indulgence, which can be earned once, on August 2 or the Sunday before or after, from noon of the previous day to the evening of the day itself. The conditions are a visit to the church, praying the Our Father and Creed, reception of the sacraments of reconciliation and Communion, and prayer for the Pope's intention, which may be a freely chosen prayer or an Our Father and Hail Mary.

Indulgences are actually a remnant of early penitential practice. It is only since the Middle Ages that individual confession has been practiced; before that there was only public penance. Anyone who had sinned grievously was excluded from the Eucharist and was given a period of time, for example, twenty or forty days, during which to prepare by fasting and prayer for reintegration into the Eucharistic community. When individual confession was introduced, absolution was given immediately after confession of sins, and the penitential works had to be done afterward; these took the place of the period of public penance. The indulgence is thus the remission of the Church's assigned period of punishment for sins whose guilt has already been forgiven. This means that the indulgence itself does not forgive sins; it is not a substitute for contrition but is a form of penance. This remission of punishment is given by Church authority out of the "Church's treasury of grace": for living persons through absolution, for the dead as a petition. Therefore personal, genuine repentance on the part of the sinner and the restoration of the damaged order, so far as possible, are always preconditions.

Pope Paul VI gave new rules for indulgences in 1967 in his apostolic constitution *Indulgentiarum Doctrina*. The essence of the indulgence is the special prayer of the Church, which is constantly being carried out in liturgical actions and in the prayer of the faithful for the complete purification of all the Church's members. This is then applied solemnly and in a special way through an indulgence granted to those who fulfill the specified conditions. As in other forms of elimination of guilt, the Church as the body of Christ prays in solidarity with its head, recalling his redemptive deeds. This is the source of what is called, not very happily, the "Church's treasury of grace"—that is, the grace won by Jesus Christ to which the Church has access. It is nothing else but God's saving will in fullness of love to individual human persons, which also includes purification and overcoming the punishment due to sin. A correct understanding of indulgences is thus very far removed from the magical ideas that may have been suggested by the practices of Luther's time.

If the whole practice is to retain any meaning, forms and symbols must be created that really provide an experience of the fact that, as Karl Rahner put it, "The Church as body of Christ and community of those on the road to salvation always intercedes for individual members whose salvation is endangered and who are sincerely seeking it." This could be experienced in the community's petitions and in penitential services. It must be clearly taught that the doctrines of the communion of saints, the veneration of saints, the punishment of sins, the necessity of personal repentance and reparation, and thus also the practice of granting indulgences stand within the context of the whole Christian life. To emphasize this, Paul VI gave twenty detailed norms for teaching about and granting indulgences. It seems doubtful that our parish communities really know of these norms—but perhaps this is simply because indulgences no longer have much importance in Catholic devotion.

Celebrating Salvation in History:
The Three Days of Easter

35

Time as Symbol: The Easter Vigil

In many parish communities, the liturgy of the Easter Vigil is begun early in the evening of Holy Saturday. Particularly when daylight saving time is in force, it is often still broad daylight. But the basic order for the Church year demands that the whole Vigil be held as a night celebration, which means that it really should not begin before darkness has fallen. What is the right time, then?

The proper choice of a time for a particular celebration already constitutes a sign of what is to be celebrated. When complaints are raised about the poverty of symbols in our liturgy, a lack of understanding for time as a fundamental category for Christian worship is certainly a major aspect of this (see ch. 9 above). The Easter night, according to the oldest traditions, is a night of watching for the Lord (cf. Exod 12:42), when the community "waits for the Lord's resurrection and celebrates it in sacred signs" (General Calendar). In the earliest Christian centuries this "mother of all vigils" (Augustine)— in a certain sense the feast of feasts in the Church's year—took all night and concluded with the common meal only when the Easter day began to dawn and the "night is made day by the resurrection of our Lord" (concluding blessing). The women, according to the Gospel reading for the Easter Vigil, come to the tomb "after the Sabbath, toward the dawn of the first day of the week" (Matt 28:1). Therefore the community today should also first "approach the table which the Lord has prepared for his people through his death and resurrection . . . when the memorial day of the resurrection approaches" (Missal). For the liturgical movement it was still clear that "from the point of view of the event itself and the meaning of the feast, there can be no more appropriate and beautiful time for beginning the Easter celebration than just before dawn, that is, about five A.M." (K. Tilmann). But in fact the tendency to anticipating the feast has grown stronger in the last ten years, so that it often appears to be just a Saturday evening Mass. This tendency was even supported by the observation that modern people tend to be evening types, more open and convivial in the evening hours.

That may be true. But the Easter Vigil is not just an evening celebration; it is a night feast. And even for "modern evening people" the night does not begin at sundown, but hours later. And this worship service is a night liturgy. If Christ is the light that shines forth through his resurrection, the morning star of the *Exultet* song, and if the community goes with him from slavery to freedom, from death to life, from night into day and from darkness to light, then the optimal time for the celebration must be near the end of the night.

Thus the decision about the time for the celebration has theological dimensions; the choice of a beginning point for the Easter Vigil is a catechetical statement that may by no means be determined solely by the question of when most people are likely to come. The structure of the celebration: light service, service of the Word, celebration of baptism, and Eucharist would fit well with a liturgy celebrated in the early morning, from the last hour of darkness (around five A.M.) to full day (around seven A.M.). Afterward, the community could gather in front of the church to sing Easter and springtime songs. A social hour with coffee in the parish center or community room should express the special nature of this day. The celebration of the Easter Mass in the forenoon does not argue against the early morning time for the Vigil. It would be fatal for the Mass on Easter Day to be more festal than the Easter Vigil Mass. Late evening is scarcely an option for this celebration if older people and children are to be present. For this group, early morning is undoubtedly better. And the sacrifice involved in getting up so early cannot really be a problem at a time when youth groups are so enthusiastic about early morning services. The contrast with Christmas can also be a reason for placing the Easter Vigil service in the morning: Christmas customs (in Germany, at least) place the accent on Christmas Eve, when presents are distributed, while at Easter the emphasis has always been put on the morning, with its Easter egg hunts and Easter parades.

There is no doubt that it would be worthwhile to try celebrating the Easter Vigil in the early morning, without regard for convenience or other seemingly practical reasons. This moment in time underscores better than any other the event that happens symbolically in the liturgy of this night.

36

The Unfolding of a Celebration as Symbol: The Structure of the Easter Vigil

The Easter Vigil service contains four units: At the beginning of the night watch the community kindles its lights (light service); in their illumination it listens to the mighty deeds of God in the readings and makes them its own through song and prayer (service of the Word). Then it incorporates new members and confesses its own baptism (baptismal service), a movement culminating in the Lord's Supper, the center of the paschal mystery (Eucharistic service). It is only too evident that, since this is the most important liturgical celebration of the whole year, we are continually thinking about the most appropriate ways of celebrating it. The structure of a service also has its own symbolic character.

So we might ask whether it would not be better to begin with the service of the Word. It very often happens that the kindling of the Easter fire remains a clerical liturgy, since the congregation is already assembled in the church; or else, if everyone has gathered around the fire, the procession into the dark church creates problems. So we could use another model, beginning with the service of the Word. There could be just enough light for the lectors to be able to read the texts. The group of celebrants would enter, beforehand, in silence, and begin the liturgy with a greeting and word of introduction. The number of readings is a secondary consideration; what is important is that the selection should be such as to cover the whole Pasch. It would also seem sensible not to sing the *Gloria* immediately after the last Old Testament reading, and also to omit the Alleluia after the reading from the New Testament. In this way, it will be clear that God is at work from the very beginning to effect the salvation that is fulfilled in the Gospel proclamation of the death and resurrection of the Messiah. Our joy at this will unfold in the light service. Now the paschal candle, perhaps accompanied by the Good Friday cross, should be brought in procession to the sanctuary, a symbolic expression of the unity of the whole mystery of the Lord's death and resurrection. After the Lord's resurrection has been proclaimed in the Gospel, the Easter candle can be lighted, so that the words of the Gospel are lifted up into symbol. During the procession which follows, the threefold *Lumen Christi* can be sung, or it may be repeated until the candles of all those present have been lighted. The Easter song of praise, the *Exultet,* should follow immediately, and the community's affirmation should be given in the Alleluia. When the voices of organ and bells are added, the response to the proclamation of the Word has reached its high point. Now the baptismal and Eucharistic celebrations may begin.

This alternative model was suggested years ago by the Regensburg liturgist Bruno Kleinheyer. It is intended to permit the meaning of this Vigil, the night-watch during the progression from darkness to light, to be more clearly illuminated by changing the order proposed by the Missal and placing the service of the Word before the light ceremony. A comparison of this alternative with the traditional form will show that no essential element is lacking; however, a number of problems that are present in the current arrangement are hereby solved. For example, it does not make any sense for the congregation to light their candles during the initial ceremony of light, then extinguish them during the service of the Word and light them again for the baptismal celebration. In the alternative model they can go on burning through the services of light and baptism. Likewise, the new questions that may arise are easily solved: the *Gloria* will probably have to go unless it is sung as a thanksgiving hymn after Communion; the homily should not be after the Gospel, since that would obscure the symbolism of the Easter candle and the procession, but it could be preached as an introduction to the renewal of baptismal vows.

We are not proposing here that one or another community should choose this alternative model as a substitute for the existing structure of the Easter Vigil. But this example shows the necessity for every community to take a more active interest in the symbols it uses in its liturgy. When the Easter Vigil is celebrated in its entirety even before nightfall on Holy Saturday evening, the symbols of a liturgy that leads us from darkness into light no longer make sense. But a celebration whose symbols do not make sense is, at best, the carrying out of a prescribed ritual and cannot express in symbolic form what the content of the celebration is supposed to be. Form and content, symbols and the faith they represent, must all agree. Obviously, this does not hold true for the Easter Vigil alone.

37

The Meaning of Light:
The Great Easter Song
of Praise (Exsultet)

In a sense we can say that the Easter Vigil opens with three different light rituals, or *lucernaria,* which are layered within one another. The light service in itself is not characteristic of Easter; it was the natural introductory procedure at every evening service in the ancient world. When light enters the darkness, God's presence is felt and we give God thanks. Thus even today the Byzantine Vespers contains an elaborate *lucernarium* rite, with the hymn *Phos Hilaron,* "O gracious light, pure brightness of the everliving Father in heaven," in which Father, Son, and Spirit are praised. Christ is the new Sun of Justice, the eternal light. Such a ritual at the beginning of our Easter liturgy is not in the immediate sense a symbol of the resurrection, for the Easter event does not occur through the lighting of a candle; Easter, the passage from death to life, begins at the moment when the deacon opens the book of the Gospels and proclaims to the whole world: "Why do you seek the living among the dead? He is not here; he has been raised" (Luke 24:5-6).

The first light ritual is the kindling of the fire, probably the remnant of a pagan custom of lighting fire in the spring. The prayer of blessing expresses longing for God, the unquenchable light. Then the Easter candle is lighted (see ch. 51 below). A second light ritual takes place in the *Lumen Christi* procession, when the burning paschal candle is carried into the church while "Christ, our Light" is sung. This, together with the passing of the light to the congregation, may remind us of Jesus' words: "I am the light of the world. Whoever fol-

115

lows me . . . will have the light of life" (John 8:12). The third of the light rituals is found in the salutation of the light in a solemn hymn, the *Exsultet,* the great Easter song of praise. The present text probably stems from the fourth century. It is true that the attribution to Ambrose of Milan (d. 397) is not certain, but this blessing of light does come from that period and region, that is, from northern Italy or southern Gaul.

The *Exsultet* begins with an introduction celebrating the joy in heaven, on earth, and in the Church but also containing an admonition to the singer. The prayer of blessing proper follows. Like the Eucharistic prayer, or any prayer of consecration, it begins with a dialogue and contains a thanksgiving for God's actions in Christ; then comes the praise of the Easter night with the repeated "This is the night." The various insertions, such as the group of four "O" phrases, indicate the great age of the text. Other elements include the presentation of the sacrifice of light ("In the joy of this night . . . receive our evening sacrifice of praise"), the praise of the candle, and of the mother bee. The hymn climaxes in an epiclesis ("May the Morning Star which never sets find this flame still burning: Christ, that Morning Star, who came back from the dead") and ends with a doxology.

Thus we may distinguish elements of a Eucharist of light: thanksgiving and its foundation in memory (anamnesis) of the saving works of God, with the Easter redemption as theme; there is no material sacrifice (such as the candle), but instead there is a spiritual sacrifice of thanksgiving and praise. There is also praise of the candle, a prayer that the symbol of the candle may have a beneficial and saving effect (epiclesis), and a concluding prayer of praise (doxology). Within this Eucharist of light, the Easter hymn of praise is incorporated as an additional element which could also easily be included in a Eucharistic prayer. The fundamental theme of the Exultet is thanksgiving and praise for the light and the event of the Easter night: redemption through the paschal mystery. All the other elements are secondary.

Despite the great beauty of this hymn, a revision of the text might well make sense in order that the thanksgiving for the resurrection of Christ, symbolized in the Easter light, and for the redemption accomplished through the Pasch would be more central. But even as it stands, it is evident how important for the liturgy are the elements of creation as symbols for the work of God.

38

Oil: Symbol of Healing and Salvation

On the eleventh Sunday in year C, the central focus of the scriptural readings is the encounter between Jesus and a sinful woman who anoints his feet with ointment (see Luke 7:36-50). In the ancient Orient it was a sign of hospitality to provide water and oil for the guests' anointing. The fact that these amenities were not provided for Jesus in the house of Simon the Pharisee shows that he was being treated in an almost hostile manner. It is as much a matter of normal practice for us as it was for people in Jesus' time to anoint ourselves with aromatic oil: We put on oil or cream after a refreshing bath or before a sun "bath," we use perfumed sprays or creams (cf. "chrism," which means "an oil for anointing") before we go to a party. In the liturgy there are anointings at baptism, confirmation, ordination, and, of course, at the anointing of the sick.

The oils used for these different anointings are blessed at a special Eucharistic celebration, the Chrism Mass presided over by the bishop in the diocesan cathedral on the morning of Holy Thursday. This was not always the case, for until the reform of Holy Week in 1956—a first, major step in liturgical reform which occurred under Pope Pius XII—the oils were blessed at the principal Mass of Holy Thursday. Of course, this Mass was then celebrated on Holy Thursday morning. With the renewal of the Easter Triduum of the Lord's Passion, Death, and Resurrection, the celebration of the Last Supper with the washing of feet was transferred to the evening, so that the sacred triduum (the three holy days) extends from the evening of Holy Thurs-

117

day to Vespers of Easter Sunday. There were probably two reasons for establishing the practice of having a Chrism Mass on Holy Thursday morning: first of all, unburdening the Last Supper commemoration of the extra ceremony of blessing of oil, and second, making it possible for all the priests of the diocese to take part in the Chrism Mass in order to express the unity of the presbyterate with the bishop. This practice was also known in the early Middle Ages. But since this time is also inconvenient for priests because of the proximity of the major liturgical celebrations in their own parishes, "the blessing may be held on an earlier day, near Easter." This sensible direction is given in the pastoral introduction to *The Rite of the Blessing of Oils*, (10).

The Chrism Mass shows in a special way that the "bishop is . . . the high priest of his flock" from whom "the life in Christ of his faithful is in some way derived" (*ibid.*, 1; *SC* 41). Every liturgical celebration is only possible in communion with and with the approval of the bishop. "The newly baptized are anointed and confirmed with the chrism consecrated by the bishop. Catechumens are prepared and disposed for baptism with the second oil. And the sick are anointed in their illness with the third oil" (*The Rite of the Blessing of Oils*, introduction, 1). In being anointed with chrism, the faithful are given a share in the royal and prophetic priestly office of Christ: Through baptism they are incorporated in the paschal mystery, and the anointing at confirmation shows that they are sealed with the Holy Spirit. The anointing with the oil of catechumens is meant to strengthen those preparing for baptism in the struggle against sin. And the anointing with the oil of the sick (cf. Jas 5:14) is a means of healing for soul and body. Olive oil or another vegetable oil serves as a common basis. The blessing of chrism is reserved to the bishop, but at an adult baptism the oil of catechumens can be blessed by the priest. This is also permitted for the oil of the sick in cases of emergency.

The oil of the sick can be blessed immediately before the conclusion of the Eucharistic prayer, and the other oils after Communion. But the conclusion of the Liturgy of the Word would be a more sensible place for both, since the proclamation of the word points toward the blessing (cf. *The Rite of the Blessing of Oils*, introduction, 12). The priests present, who concelebrate with the bishop, cooperate with him when they stretch out their hands at the blessing of chrism. They ask the power of God for that which they and the bishop will do in sacred signs at baptism, confirmation, and anointing of the sick.

It would certainly be desirable for the importance of the symbol of holy oil to receive more emphasis in the parish community. These oils could, for example, be carried in the entrance procession on Holy Thursday and receive a special place during the celebration of the Lord's Supper. We might also consider the possibility of reserving them visibly in the church in a kind of tabernacle. Two theology students from Cologne wrote on this subject in connection with a proposal by Theodor Schnitzler:

> That would certainly be a very beautiful and expressive custom. It would be quite supportive of the reverence due to the sacraments whose administration is connected with an anointing. But it would be possible in all churches to give more expression to the connection of these sacraments with the Eucharist, the center of all liturgy.

In this way the meaning of oil as a symbol of healing and salvation could be more clearly expressed in our communities.

39

The Foot Washing: An Incomprehensible Symbol?

The evening of Holy Thursday is characterized by the celebration of the love of the Lord, which is given as a basic motif in the Gospel reading (John 13:1): "Having loved his own who were in the world, he loved them to the end." The liturgical celebration which begins the days of Easter symbolizes this love of Christ in cross, supper, and foot washing. Thereby it is made clear that this evening is already leading toward Good Friday. While the first reading describes Israel's paschal feast (see Exod 12) and the second gives Paul's account of the institution of the Lord's supper (see 1 Cor 11), the Gospel, in the story of Jesus washing his disciples' feet (see John 13:1-5), indicates what must determine the life of the community if it wants to remain united with the Body and Blood of the Lord in the supper: mutual service to one another! Thus the liturgy on this evening expresses in a particularly persuasive way that *martyria* (proclaiming the faith), *liturgia* (celebrating the faith), and *diakonia* (doing the faith) have to be inseparably united. The rite of foot washing following this reading is intended to give symbolic expression, in a kind of brief drama, to what has been proclaimed. But does this symbol say anything? Does it express today what it really means? Apparently those responsible for the revision of the rites were not entirely sure, since the Missal says, "Depending on pastoral circumstances, the washing of feet follows the homily." Most pastors seem to be of the opinion that their circumstances do not make the foot washing advisable, and they omit it. Here we have to do with a symbol which, from its origins, really has the characteristics of a sacrament; in any case it is directly traceable, as are few others, to an action of Jesus.

But as early as the beginning of the 1970s, the conference of liturgists and church musicians in Switzerland had decided "that the washing of feet is no longer to be recommended, since it represents a pure ritualization of Christ's command of service, which is problematic in itself and finds less and less response today." In its stead "another contemporary symbol of love" should be inserted. A survey revealed that only thirteen percent of German parishes use this rite.

But is this symbol really so incomprehensible? Or is it perhaps only a question of an appropriate way of doing it? Is this not just as true of the water of baptism or bread and wine or the oil of the sick? There are some really basic questions at issue here: Invented signs often point to what is secondary rather than to the center of the celebration, Christ; whereas the traditional symbols may be difficult to understand but for that very reason cause us to reflect on them. I do not want to discuss at this point the suggestions made for alternative signs, which have been tried here and there with more or less success. The fact that the washing of feet, when properly done, can still "speak" to us is shown by a pastor from Bruchsal, writing in the magazine *Gottesdienst*. In his parish the action is done for the fathers of first communicants. It is carefully prepared through parents' evenings, home visits, and in First Communion instruction. And "so that it may be evident that the pastor, as a disciple of the Lord, should be someone who serves everyone, the whole foot washing is done while kneeling, as a sign of his bowing down before the people of his parish." In fact, this symbol speaks in the first place to the priest and underscores the service character of his office. In this parish it has been shown "that this acknowledgment of apostolate has elicited ongoing positive effects in families."

The washing of feet is to clarify and bring to our consciousness the Lord's "last will and testament": "A new commandment I give to you, that you love one another; even as I have loved you, that you also love one another" (John 13:34; antiphon for the rite). Every community should consider whether—appropriately performed and expanded through other gestures, for example, the collection for the poor of the Third World is recommended on this evening—the washing of feet would not be a visible interpretation of the saving work of Christ, who "has not come to be served, but to serve" (Matt 20:28).

40

Veneration of the Cross: The Center of the Good Friday Liturgy

The liturgy for Good Friday is now divided into three parts: the Liturgy of the Word, consisting of readings and petitions; the veneration of the cross; and the Communion service. The first of these is the oldest form, going back to about the fourth century. The veneration of the cross, taken over from Jerusalem where people were understandably interested in shaping the ceremonies to suit the place, was then added, and the Communion service was introduced still later. The Liturgy of the Word is clearly constructed, with its emphasis on the Passion according to John, which already points toward the Easter Vigil: the Crucified One appears as the king and victor who accomplishes for us the passage from death to life (see John 18:1–19:42). From this point of view we can understand the succeeding veneration of the cross and Communion: The veneration of the cross is not merely a silent viewing of Christ's suffering but an impressive ceremony of honor done to the king, while the Communion service is a sharing in Christ's death and resurrection.

The service of the Word on Good Friday takes up a large block of time at the beginning, especially if the community is not sufficiently included, either as readers or singers of the Passion. They could certainly participate more: through quiet pauses, with slides; with texts for meditation distributed beforehand; through congregational singing of hymns that use parts of the Passion story, etc. The ten solemn prayers which follow need not all be used; in any case, it is certainly possible that they can be actualized in view of the situation of the particular community so as to increase attention. If the invitation to prayer and the statement of the intention are done in such a way as to awaken the interest of the congregation, the quiet moment of prayer between kneeling and standing—which should be of an appropriate length—can easily be given content.

A rearrangement of the order could also enliven the proceedings, especially since the proclamation in the readings points toward the veneration of the cross. Since, in the new order of things, we now administer sacraments and even sacramentals after the reading of the Gospel, the veneration of the cross could follow directly after the Passion, and the prayers could be said afterward, with the cross in view. This appears to be a persuasive way of including the veneration within the liturgy as a whole, and the community could be more active. Following the Passion and the homily, the cross ritual would offer an optical and meditative, even hymnic, unfolding (through the singing of the cantor and the congregation) and a making present of what has been heard. This would then, finally, come to a conclusion in the petitions, with their uniquely universal point of view.

But the cross ritual itself could be made more vigorous. Two items are decisive: Everyone, that is, the whole congregation, must take part; and there should be no differentiation between the form used by the clerics (and altar servers) and that of everyone else. As regards the form, the Missal says that all "approach to venerate the cross . . . [with] a simple genuflection or . . . some other appropriate sign of reverence. . . ." And here again it is extremely important that it be made possible for each individual to approach the Crucified One interiorly with the greatest intimacy—something which is expressed through the external sign. This cannot mean "racing past" as quickly as possible with a quick genuflection! And here each community can use its imagination: In some places the cross may be, for example, wound with barbed wire on which are hung the petitions of individuals (some of which, in turn, are read at Easter). Elsewhere, flowers are placed before the cross and are then strewn on the route of the Easter procession. Or one may, while genuflecting, touch the wounded feet with the right hand and then cross oneself. In a parish in Paderborn, a brief written introduction to the liturgy is distributed beforehand, which says, among other things:

> In the great petitions we extend our prayer over Church and world, Christians and non-Christians; Jesus Christ has died for all; he desires to bring the whole of creation to the Father. In the five stations of the veneration of the cross our thoughts carry us to all five parts part of the earth. Today also, the cross is raised, visibly and tangibly, among us.

A book is provided in which, during the period of "resting in the grave" individual "crosses" can be inscribed.

The veneration of the cross is an excellent example for showing that the rubrics in the liturgical books offer a minimum of absolutes in order that the liturgical symbols may be appropriately presented. But we need not stop with the minimum. There is enough space left for the community to shape these symbols in such a way that they can express what they are intended to signify in a manner that is particularly poignant and clear in the special situation of each community.

EXPRESSIVE BODILY ACTIONS

41

Standing, Sitting, Kneeling

There are strikingly few rules given in the Missal for the postures of the congregation. And that is understandable if we consider that the Missal is intended for the use of communities all over the world. The Instruction devotes only a few lines to this subject (GIRM 20–22). These emphasize above all that the "uniformity [in posture] observed by all taking part is a sign of the community and the unity of the assembly" and that in this way the "spiritual attitude of those taking part" is expressed and fostered. Thus, it is the responsibility of individual countries to "adapt" these basic rules "to the customs of the people. But the conference must make sure that such adaptations correspond to the meaning and character of each part of the celebration."

Standing expresses reverence but also joy, a readiness to hear and to be on the way. It is the attitude of those keeping watch. Therefore, for early Christianity this was the normal posture for prayer and worship (cf. Luke 18:11; 22:46). At the same time, this upright posture makes the future present (cf. Rev 7:9). That is why kneeling is out of order on Sundays, during the fifty days of the Easter season, and during the Eucharist. Standing is a typical Easter attitude, since liberation from sin and death through the paschal mystery of Christ has freed the community from slavery, and therefore it need no longer adopt any kind of submissive attitude. Standing is also the posture of those who await the return of Christ, for before the Son of Man only those will stand erect who have nothing to fear from his justice (cf. Mal 3:2). And, finally, the chosen in heaven stand and give thanks (see Rev 7:9; 15:2).

In the Eastern liturgies even today, the deacon, at important points in the liturgy, calls on the congregation to stand together in a reverent attitude. It was only with the change in perception in the West, whereby the liturgy became a business for clerics in which the faithful no longer took an active part, that standing was increasingly reserved for those serving at the altar. The laity, who from the Middle Ages onward were reduced to private prayer even during the Mass, preferred to kneel. Standing remained only as a gesture of respect at the entrance and exit of the clerics and during the proclamation of the Gospel.

The new Missal therefore expresses the desire that standing should regain its importance in the Eucharistic celebration. It is the expected attitude from the initial hymn through the opening prayer (collect), at the Alleluia before the Gospel, during the proclamation of the Gospel, during the Creed and prayer of the faithful, and from the prayer over the offerings until the end of the celebration. The second Eucharistic prayer says expressly: "We thank you for counting us worthy to stand in your presence and serve you."

Sitting is the attitude for meditation and listening, and is witnessed for those listening to preaching from an early date (see Acts 20:9). It is also the posture of the teacher and "pre-sider" (*prae-sedere:* to sit before). Thus the bishop directs the liturgy from his chair *(cathedra),* and the priest presides from his chair over the Liturgy of the Word and the conclusion of the Mass. The pulpit used to be called a "preaching chair" *(Predigtstuhl)* in German, which seems to indicate that it has not been very long since preachers used to sit, too. The new Missal directs that we be seated during the readings before the Gospel, the responsorial psalm, the homily, and the preparation of the gifts, and in the silent period after Communion.

As regards kneeling, on the other hand, the Instruction only says: "[The people] should kneel at the consecration unless prevented by the lack of space, the number of people present, or some other good reason" (GIRM 21). Kneeling, which was taken over in the Roman liturgy from German custom, expresses humility, penance, and adoration. To pray while kneeling is a common human custom which is also reported of Jesus (see Mark 14:35; Luke 22:41). When we kneel or prostrate ourselves, we express our lowliness before God. It is an honor paid to the ruler, as in the veneration of the cross on Good Friday. But it arises primarily from a consciousness of our own sinfulness and so characterizes penitential prayers and urgent petitions. Consequently, it is rather the exception than the rule in community liturgies, while it remains probably the most common posture for individual, private prayer. Emil J. Lengeling even says: "Our customary kneeling during the words, 'Christ has died . . .' after the consecration and until the concluding doxology is not appropriate to the character of the acclamation nor to the priestly dignity of the community, which are expressed in the memorial, offering, and praise." The Western custom of kneeling in reverence for the Eucharist during the words of consecration and when receiving Communion is, in any case, relatively recent. Since the Communion procession and receiving Communion in the hand scarcely allow for kneeling, standing to receive Communion has again become a matter of course in our parishes. Should this same posture be considered for the Eucharistic prayer as well?

Sitting and kneeling are not a matter of indifference: They are symbolic bodily expressions of what we are doing in faith at each particular moment.

42

The "Little" Sign of the Cross

The sign of the cross is first mentioned in the middle of the second century in connection with reception of the Eucharist. Shortly thereafter, Tertullian (d. after 220) gives assurance that the sign of the cross stems from apostolic tradition. He says: "At every step, when going in and out, when putting on clothes and shoes, when washing ourselves, when kindling the lights, when going to sleep, sitting down, and in every action we place the sign of the cross on our foreheads." For Augustine (d. 430), making the sign of the cross on oneself is a Christian's external confession of faith. In its original meaning it is a sign of possession: at baptism, Christ, through this sign of victory, laid his hand on the one being baptized, who received the cross traced on the forehead just as in antiquity slaves had a mark of ownership branded on their foreheads. For this reason, in the first Christian centuries the cross was simply traced on the forehead with one finger of the right hand. In the same way, at least since the fourth century, people often signed their foreheads and eyes with the Eucharistic species, especially with the consecrated wine. Alcuin, in the eighth century, mentions signing the lips.

The congregation's crossing themselves when the Gospel is announced is one of the oldest folk customs attached to the Eucharistic celebration. The desire to grasp the Word of God and hold fast to its blessing finds an enduring expression in this signing with the cross. In the ninth century, we hear for the first time that the faithful make a cross on their foreheads after the deacon's greeting. Then, a century later, we learn that the deacon and all those present, after the words "Jesus said"—that is, at the point when the Lord's voice is made present—make a cross on forehead and breast. Then, in the eleventh century, forehead, mouth, and breast are mentioned: the so-called little sign of the cross, which has become common practice since the twelfth century. Johannes Beleth, a liturgist from that period, gives a succinct explanation: "I am not ashamed of the gospel [whereby the forehead is regarded as the locus of shame]; I confess it with my lips and in my heart." The original sense of the sign of the cross at the Gospel reading would probably have been that it is a protection and help toward a proper encounter with the sacred Word. From the same period we also find mention of the signing of the book of the Gospels with the cross. Again, at the conclusion of the Gospel proclamation, the congregation are accustomed to cross themselves again. To explain this cross at the end of the reading, the medieval commentators applied the passage about the enemy who tries to take the seed of the Word of God out of the hearers' hearts (see Luke 8:12). The signing before the beginning of the Gospel, the only one that has survived to the present day, was first explained in a similar fashion and thus represented a kind of self-blessing. Later it was increasingly interpreted in terms of readiness for courageous confession in the Pauline sense: "For I am not ashamed of the gospel" (Rom 1:16).

> It is probably in this sense that, beginning with a crossing of the forehead, there developed a threefold sign of the cross, plus the signing of the book: we want to stand up with bold faces for the word that Christ brought us and which is written in this book, to confess it with our lips, but especially to preserve it faithfully in our hearts (J. A. Jungmann).

What the spirit accepts the lips should confess, and the inner person should take it to heart. Thus, the little sign of the cross is an admirable custom, deeply anchored in traditions of piety that go back a thousand years. For this reason the new Missal has also retained it: When the deacon or priest exchanges the greeting, "The Lord be with you. And with your spirit" with the community and then announces, "A reading from the holy Gospel according to . . . ," he makes the sign of the cross on the book and then on his forehead, lips, and breast.

The large, or Latin, cross, tracing the beams of the cross from the forehead to the lower breast and from the left to the right shoulder, came into general liturgical use rather late. However, it is occasionally mentioned as early as the sixth century and again in the eleventh.

43

Striking the Breast

The symbol of striking one's breast is certainly another of the very ancient gestures in our liturgy. It is founded in Scripture, especially in the example of the Pharisee and the tax collector in the Temple. The former preens himself before God, that is, he does exactly the opposite of striking his breast. "But the tax collector, standing far off, would not even lift up his eyes to heaven, but beat his breast, saying, 'God be merciful to me a sinner!' " (Luke 18:13; cf. also 23:48). This sign is thus a form of humility, of self-deprecation, and in the early Church was seen as an expression of penitence. Since the heart is regarded as the source and seat of sin, this sign can be understood in biblical terms as a visible expression of a genuine consciousness of sin.

The preconciliar order of Mass prescribed that the priest should strike his breast three times during the *Confiteor*. Since that Ordo, in contrast to our present Missal, contained instructions only for the priest and the community was not mentioned at all, there was no instruction for the congregation at this point. For centuries they were condemned to remain spectators. But it was a logical development that, first of all, the altar servers, who represent the congregation, struck their breasts as the priest did. And in recent times, when the congregation had Missals and could follow the course of the Mass, they also began to strike their breasts at this point. The priest was also to strike his breast at other points during the Mass: at the next-to-last section of the Eucharistic prayer (Roman canon) at the words "To us also, your sinful servants . . ."; three times during the *Agnus Dei;* three times at the "Lord, I am not worthy." There were no instructions for the congregation at these points either, but everyone who was present at the time will remember that the people imitated the priest. There were also some people who used to make this sign while genuflecting on entering or leaving the pew, and three times after the words of consecration.

What is the custom today? It is prescribed that, at the confession of sins, all should strike their breasts at the words "I have sinned in thought, word, and deed, through my fault, through my fault, through my most grievous fault." That is, this is now for the first time ordered for the congregation, even though they used to do it without being instructed to do so. The Instruction probably has in mind only a single gesture. Of course, the text implies that one should strike one's breast three times, but here as everywhere it is certainly true that less can be more.

For the first Eucharistic prayer it is merely said that the priest strikes his breast once with the right hand. Since he speaks this prayer in the name of the congregation, his gesture should be sufficient for all.

According to the new Ordo, neither the celebrant nor the congregation strikes the breast during the *Agnus Dei*. We should probably regard the earlier practice as not especially appropriate. The "Lamb of God" is a song accompanying the breaking of the bread. And if the priest were really to break the bread for the whole community and not only his single, large host, he could not at the same time make the sign of striking his breast. Of course, the community could do so. But we can object that a gesture at each strophe of this song does not seem very practical. Thus we should probably maintain the position that striking the breast at the *Agnus Dei* has scarcely any meaning and therefore has appropriately been discarded.

There remains, then, only the *Confiteor,* when priest and congregation confess their guilt, through words and signs, in solidarity before God and one another. "I am a sinner," said Augustine in one of his sermons. "Together with you, I beat my breast, with you I beg for forgiveness, with you I hope that God will be gracious to me." "Those who, in the attitude of the publican, strike their breasts and confess their guilt, may then hear the Word of God and celebrate the sacred mysteries in the company of Jesus' disciples" (B. Kleinheyer).

44

The Sign of Peace

"**P**eace be with you!" was the greeting given, according to John's Gospel, by the post-Easter Lord on the evening of the day of his resurrection to the disciples who were gathered behind closed doors "for fear of the Jews." It is the salvation promised in this greeting that has the power to deliver the community from fear and to make possible its mission to the world: "Peace be with you. As the Father has sent me, even so I send you" (John 20:21). So being a Christian means being gifted with the peace of God, being called to obtain God's salvation, and so to proclaim this peace to the world.

Thus it practically goes without saying that the realization of this promise of peace in the present moment was, from the very beginning, a prominent part of the Sunday assembly of the Christians. It could even be said to represent a climax. Originally the greeting of peace was exchanged before the Eucharistic prayer, and it still has that place in the Eastern Churches. When the prayers of intercession were concluded, "they greeted each other with a holy kiss" (Justin, d. after 150). Then the Eucharistic gifts were brought forward. The transfer of the greeting to a point just before Communion began in North Africa and extended throughout the West in the fourth and fifth centuries. The connection between the greeting of peace and the Communion was later so strong in many places that, as reception of Communion declined, it was even regarded as a substitute for Communion itself.

The new emphasis on the importance of the gesture of extending peace to one another, which we find in the renewed order of Mass, is intended to show that Communion is to be understood not only as a union with Christ, the head, but also with his body, our sisters and brothers in Christ. The greeting thus underscores the horizontal dimension of the Lord's Supper. It is not just a matter of one's own individual salvation but of the good of the whole community and, ultimately, of all humankind.

The moment has three parts: The priest petitions Jesus Christ, in the name of the community, for peace; he then extends that peace to the whole assembly; the assembly realizes this wish in the sign of greeting. Even earlier, in the embolism of the Our Father, the priest asks, "Give us peace in our day." He then introduces the gesture of peace with words that are adapted, as far as possible, to the current situation; for example, in the Easter season: "On the day of Easter Jesus stood in the midst of his disciples and said: 'Peace be with you.' Therefore we pray . . . ." Then he extends his hands to the congregation and says, "The peace of the Lord be with you always," thus asking them to give a sign of their readiness to be reconciled with one another.

It is a pleasure to see that, in more and more communities, the common isolation of individuals is interrupted by this greeting of peace—if only through a handshake with the neighbors on each side, in front, and behind. When we have looked into someone's eyes in this way, we will also greet that person outside the church and take an interest in him or her. Many congregations (at least occasionally) go beyond this: They exchange flowers or bind single flowers together into a big bunch; or people are invited to converse with their neighbors for two minutes; or slips on which addresses are written, and which had been collected during the preparation of the gifts, are distributed, and after Mass each person meets his or her "draw" for a chat in the parish hall. For no one can extend peace to her- or himself. In this greeting each member of the community acknowledges that she or he is one of those who are sent to bring peace and to share the sufferings of others.

It is hardly surprising that many people find it hard to shake the hands of others, often strangers to them, at the greeting of peace. The body can only express what our inner attitude really is. Christians who regard the Eucharistic celebration—as they were taught to do before the Council—as something that takes place between God and each individual present are not inwardly prepared to genuinely interact with others during the service. The more the liturgy is recognized as a community action, the easier it will be to wish one another God's peace not only in our hearts but in outward gestures as well. Young people brought up in the spirit of the Council experience very few problems in this regard.

45

The Liturgical Kiss: An Alienating Symbol?

If Alfred Lorenzer (see ch. 7 above) was correct in saying that the Council had destroyed the sensuousness of liturgy (or better, its appeal to the senses) and replaced symbols with words and uninterrupted instruction, then there would be no more room for kisses in the liturgy. It is certainly true that there is scarcely any element that is so firmly located in the realm of the senses as a kiss exchanged between persons, and even from person to thing. But we can say categorically that the tradition of the liturgical kiss has not only been retained but has even received a new lease on life. Of course, the kissing of objects is somewhat problematic in our day and age. There were plenty of voices in favor of eliminating this gesture, and it is true that many priests have trouble with it. But in fact, the kissing of the altar at the beginning of the Eucharistic celebration (GIRM 27; 232) and after the final blessing (GIRM 125) is obligatory. The same is true of the kissing of the Lectionary after the reading of the gospel (GIRM 95; 232). Certainly, a bishops' conference could prescribe another gesture of reverence if this one is not appropriate to the feelings or traditions of the people in a particular place (GIRM 232). I do not want to enter into a discussion of whether our sensibilities are more or less alienated by the kissing of objects, even the altar or the Lectionary. It can scarcely be disputed that such a gesture, if it is done properly, is a sign appealing to the senses.

Obviously, kisses exchanged between persons, such as the kiss of peace, are more meaningful. Before the Council, the kiss of peace was only exchanged, in a highly ritualized and spiritualized form, among the clergy, while the rest of the congregation could at most, in accordance with the rubrics of the Missal of 1570, kiss a plate handed around before Communion. It is true that the renewed Missal does not speak of a kiss but rather of a greeting of peace. But the precise nature of the sign by which mutual peace is to be extended and brotherly/ sisterly love expressed is not laid down (GIRM 112). Yet we have heard from other countries, and even from many liturgies in our own land, that bodiliness can play a major role at this point, and even take the form of kisses exchanged, so that "it is no longer so necessary to encourage people to accept the invitation, as much as to restrain the excess of emotion that breaks out at this point in the postconciliar Mass" (B. Fischer).

The old tradition of the kiss of welcome, given to the newly ordained at the conclusion of episcopal, priestly, and diaconal ordination ceremonies by those already installed in the corresponding office, has been revived. What could give a clearer and more sense-oriented expression of their reception into their new status? The same can be said for this gesture at the time of profession into a religious order.

But let me return to the question of kissing objects. In order to restore to the kissing of the altar its meaning as a greeting and farewell and a sign of reverence, "all the kisses of the altar that have been introduced into the Mass in the course of centuries (e.g., the kiss before every turn toward the people) have to be eliminated. . . . Other liturgical kisses had to be dropped, because people today find them to be unbearably ceremonious or an expression of excessive devotion" (B. Fischer). This applies, for example, to kissing the stole while vesting in the sacristy, kissing the bishop's ring before receiving Communion, and kissing liturgical vessels and instruments before handing them to the celebrant. Kissing the pope's foot at papal ceremonies has also been eliminated.

Certainly, the liturgical kiss is not a particularly central symbol within the liturgical language of gestures. But this small slice of liturgical action can serve to show that, at least as far as the text of the liturgical books is concerned, there can be no talk of a loss of bodiliness or appeal to the senses in our liturgy.

46

Play and Dance:
Bodily Symbols of Faith

If liturgical celebration is supposed to address the whole person, bodily forms of expression are an integral part of it. We are perfectly clear about that as regards such actions as standing, sitting, kneeling, and walking. But in our region we can still scarcely imagine that a parish liturgy could include play and dancing. And yet, in the early Church such practices were widespread. Mainly because of the connection between dancing and pagan cult, the ancient Church gradually turned against liturgical dance. But since dancing is an expression of joy and is a natural part of the celebration of festivals, it persisted in various forms, even in face of express prohibitions, down to the end of the Middle Ages. There are remnants even today, such as the springtime procession in Echternach or the dance before the exposed Eucharist in the cathedral of Seville. Since dance can also be described as stylized, rhythmically ordered movement, festive processions can be regarded as types of dancing even today. And certain liturgies that are imbued with joy, such as those at national Catholic congresses, often end in spontaneous dancing. The renewed liturgy in Africa, for example, is making a conscious effort to integrate native forms of dance. In our country this is generally reserved for children's liturgies and youth Masses, but in these cases it is officially recommended, as in *The Directory for Masses with Children*. It is especially popular as a response to the readings or at the preparation of the gifts, when play and dance are often combined.

Play and dance can serve as elements of visualization and activation. They can prepare for the proclamation of the message, clarify

141

it, and prolong it into daily life. As regards play in children's liturgies, this fact has long been recognized; the literature on the subject is immense. There is a basis for the revival of liturgical forms of dance in the Constitution on the Liturgy, which suggests the possibility that the "spiritual adornments and gifts of the various races and peoples" that are not "indissolubly bound up with superstition and error" may be integrated into the liturgy (SC 37). Several forms should be distinguished. There is representative dance, which is not a show, but a depiction of actions or feelings done in such a way that the congregation dances inwardly with the performers. Possible moments for this would be penitential acts or proclamation of the Word. Then there is dance as prayer, perhaps as the congregation's response to the Word of God or to prayers and songs, such as the Our Father. Another possibility is community dancing, for which we have little or no traditional basis in our liturgy. It is usually spontaneous, as we see especially in youth services. The greeting of peace is an appropriate moment for this, as well as the time after Communion and the dismissal. The procession could well be the conclusion of a representative dance and thus form a transition to the service of Word and sacrament. Finally, there is meditative dance, which seems especially appropriate for small groups.

Certainly we cannot force forms of dance and play on normal Sunday liturgies. But any community that celebrates together ought to give some thought to the question of how it can use physical forms of expression to give its liturgies a festal character.

PLACES FOR WORSHIP ACTIVITIES

47

The Altar as Symbol
of the Eucharistic Celebration

In The General Instruction of the Roman Missal (259), the meaning of the altar is described in this way: "At the altar the sacrifice of the cross is made present under sacramental signs. It is also the table of the Lord and the people of God are called together to share in it. The altar is, as well, the center of the thanksgiving that the Eucharist accomplishes."

This paragraph contains a wealth of theological statement, the most important aspect of which is the fact that the Christian altar has nothing to do with the sacrificial altars of other cults. The sacramental sign of the Mass is not a sacrificial ritual, but an act of thanksgiving, the Eucharist over bread and wine, the elements of the meal "which in themselves represent the sacrificed, self-surrendering Lord; they rest upon the altar, which we should preferably—in order to avoid any misunderstandings rooted in the study of comparative religions—and more justly call the *mensa Domini*, the table of the Lord" (J. H. Emminghaus).

The fundamental form of the Christian altar is thus not a mighty sacrificial stone but a table. In early times it was brought into the room for each liturgical celebration. Although we still find evidence of wooden tables as late as the eighth century, fixed altars of stone were on the increase after the fourth century, not least because of the symbolic equation of the altar with Christ, the rock (see 1 Cor 10:4), the cornerstone (see 1 Pet 2:7; Eph 2:20), the living stone (see 1 Pet 2:4). The altar table was usually, until as late as the seventh century, only about a yard square, since only the bread and wine, the Scriptures, and the liturgical text were laid upon it. Only in the seventh to eighth centuries did the table form retreat in favor of a block or cubic shape because, among other reasons, relics were now being placed within the altar. From this point it was no great step to the notion of the altar as a grave for relics, "which inspired the Renaissance to make altars in the form of sarcophagi, a highly questionable invention, if we consider the original function of the holy table" (A. Adam). From that period reliquaries and receptacles for Communion to be carried to the sick were placed on the altar; from the eleventh century the cross was added, as well as two candlesticks—a custom that became obligatory with the Missal of 1570. Since the sixteenth century the high altar has increasingly been combined with the tabernacle. Beginning with the early Middle Ages, the altar was built closer to the rear wall of the apse, and the sanctuary that was thus created was separated from the congregation by means of a railing or other barrier. Thus the retable-altar developed, with a painted background at the rear side of the altar; this in turn led to the building up of the back of the altar itself. The Gothic period expanded this into a winged altar, and the baroque produced complete stage settings.

> Modeling the altar on pagan sacrificial stones is a modern and recent development. Certainly, the Eucharistic celebration is also a representation of Christ's sacrifice, which the Church is entitled to make its own and into which it enters. But this is a sacrificial celebration in a different sense from that of Jewish and pagan sacrifices—so much so that early Christian writers emphasized that "we Christians have no altars (sacrificial stones) and no sacrifices." . . . From this point of view it is clear that every shape that departs from the form and symbolism of the table can only be secondary and may never be used to obscure what is uniquely Christian in the Eucharistic celebration (E. J. Lengeling).

Thus history provides us with standards which we ought to respect. Too often, secondary elements have determined liturgical forms, to the detriment of the primary symbolism.

"The Christian altar is by its very nature a table of sacrifice and at the same time a table of the paschal banquet," according to *The Renewed Rite for the Dedication of an Altar* (draft version of 1981). It is the "table of the Lord" (GIRM 259), so that "the table form is the only legitimate one" (J. H. Emminghaus). It is the "center of the thanksgiving" toward which other liturgical services are, in a certain sense, ordered. Therefore it should stand free, in the center of the worship space. It is presupposed that it is possible to move around it: "In every church there should ordinarily be a fixed, dedicated altar, which should be freestanding to allow the ministers to walk around it easily and Mass to be celebrated facing the people. It should be so placed as to be a focal point on which the attention of the whole congregation centers naturally" (GIRM 262).

Do the form and placement of the altar in our churches really correspond to these instructions? J. E. Mayer, a parish priest in the city of Vienna, rightly complains:

> Look at everything that has piled up on it in the last few years! It has almost turned into a pedestal again. And the things lying on it are even more visible than they used to be, when they tended to disappear in the perspective of the whole edifice. People are uneasy about the emptiness of modern churches, and uncomfortable with the emptiness of the silent altar of sacrifice. And so it gets tricked out and decorated. Six tall, thick candles on massive candelabra and a cross, all standing in a row, create a new rood-screen on the altar itself. They are like a dividing wall screening the celebrant and the gifts from the people. Nobody can really see what is on the altar and which objects are most important. The handicrafts of worthy parishioners and staff are overrunning the altar. Add to that a microphone and the big Missal on a massive, angled wooden stand. Would you believe it, there are even a chalice and paten on the altar, too! Is that the way it should be? Is this really what the liturgical reform intended?

In fact, what should be on the altar table are first of all the gifts, which are inconspicuous and under no circumstances ought to be made visually insignificant by unimportant odds and ends. It is a question of an order of importance among symbols! Therefore Mayer suggests:

> The Missal lies on the middle of the altar, directly in front of the priest (a stand is unnecessary), and in front of it, on the people's side, lies the corporal with the chalice and a dish for hosts, which should not be too shallow, on it. (A paten is not appropriate, because the congre-

gation cannot see it.) Beside the book stands an inconspicuous microphone. The candles are designed as processional lights and stand near the sides of the altar. Flowers are placed on the floor near the altar, but not directly in front of it. If candles and flowers are set on the altar, they must be designed as table decorations; that is, their size and arrangement should remain modest. The crucifix should ideally be a processional cross placed near the altar. When no liturgy is being celebrated, the altar is bare, just as is a dinner table apart from mealtimes, and like the altar of sacrifice before and after the offering. It awaits the sacred action. The open Bible should not be placed on the altar, but on the ambo, which is the "altar of the Word."

Here we have a precise and practical summary of what the theology of the Eucharistic celebration demands for the configuration of altars. Functionality and dignity are complementary aspects of the one altar: "In new churches it is better to erect one altar only, so that in the one assembly of the people of God the one altar may signify our one Savior Jesus Christ and the one Eucharist of the Church" (*Rite for the Dedication of an Altar,* introduction 7). It consists of a tabletop with a fixed base (GIRM 263), and its material should be "solid, becoming, and well crafted." A fixed altar is recommended, but a portable one is in principle admissible (GIRM 260). This applies to spaces devoted exclusively to worship; in other places "a suitable table may be used."

Thus what is decisive in the design of an altar is the expression of its primary symbolic quality—as "table of the Lord" and "center of the thanksgiving" (GIRM 259). In addition, it should be "so placed as to be a focal point on which the attention of the whole congregation centers naturally" (GIRM 262).

Many of our existing churches were designed as processional churches, in which the priest is seen at the head of the wandering people of God, with their eyes directed toward the East, to a mysterious presence in the tabernacle set up high on an impressive retable. But now that we have recognized that the altar is the place "around which" we assemble, it must be moved toward the congregation, for example, to the intersection of the nave. In many places this results in a kind of "hole" behind the altar, since the old choir appears to have no further function.

There seems to be an increasingly successful movement to close this optical gap through the erection of a retable in the choir. There is no objection in principle to such a solution, so long as the altar of celebration is not thereby forced out of its function as that which calls the community together. It will be necessary to consider, in individual cases, how one ought to proceed in this dilemma. Another solution to the problem would be a large suspended cross, or something similar, in the former choir. But we should simply indicate that both points ought to remain in view and the centrality of the altar, which has been emphasized by bringing it forward, must not be optically minimized again (H. J. Spital).

It is frequently asked whether relics are to be placed in the altar, as before. This custom, according to GIRM 266, "is to be maintained. Care must be taken to have solid evidence of the authenticity of such relics." Here we have something new: The addition of relics is no longer a requirement, but when relics "of martyrs or other saints" are introduced, they should be genuine, for "it is better for an altar to be dedicated without relics than to have relics of doubtful credibility placed beneath it," according to *The Rite for the Dedication of an Altar* (introduction 11). It is also explained at this point that we have to do with a symbol of the second order of importance: "The entire dignity of the altar consists in this: The altar is the table of the Lord. It is not, then, the bodies of the martyrs that render the altar glorious; it is the altar that renders the burial place of the martyrs glorious" (introduction 5). If the custom is retained, the place of reposition should be made evident and visible.

It is certainly a good solution, in the case of an altar in the shape of a table, to place them under the table, so that, for example, on the feast of the saint in question the place may be adorned with flowers. Occasionally the relics are reserved in the stipes (base of the altar). Thus there are no narrow limits placed on these arrangements (H. J. Spital).

Fixed altars are dedicated (GIRM 265):

[But] the celebration of the Eucharist is the most important rite, and the only necessary one, for the dedication of an altar. Nevertheless, in accordance with the common tradition of the Church, both East and West, a special prayer of dedication is also said. This prayer declares the intention of dedicating the altar to the Lord for all times, and it asks for his blessing *(Rite for the Dedication of an Altar,* introduction 21).

From its very nature, the altar is dedicated to God alone; for this reason "in new churches statues and pictures of saints may not be placed over the altar. Likewise relics of saints should not be placed on the table of the altar when they are exposed for the veneration of the people" *(ibid.* 10).

48

The Place for Proclamation

"The dignity of the Word of God requires the church to have a place that is suitable for proclamation of the Word and is a natural focal point for the people during the Liturgy of the Word. As a rule the lectern or ambo should be stationary" (GIRM 272). And since the service of the Word and of the Eucharist represent two parts of a single celebration, which are "so closely connected that they form but one single act of worship" (GIRM 8), the introduction to the Lectionary 32 reads: "Therefore every church should seek a solution whereby ambo and altar correspond to one another and stand in a correct relationship to one another."

But what is a "correct relationship"? Christ is present not only in the Eucharistic species but also in the community, and especially in his Word. The consequence of this insight is that the service of the Word is conducted at the ambo, just as the Eucharist is performed at the altar. Ambo and altar should be carefully differentiated, for every symbol functions more clearly in isolation than when mixed with others. In any case there is no indication of the exact location for the ambo. "It will always be necessary to proceed on the basis of the space at hand and to make the best of it, when it is not possible to construct a new building. But history offers us a nearly exhaustive variety of possibilities. It offers a welcome paradigm for our deliberations" (J. H. Emminghaus).

In the early days of Christian worship, the presider's seat was probably the natural place for proclamation. In ancient times it was customary for a teacher to sit on a chair and for the students to stand around him or her. In house churches, the speaker could be heard and understood from his or her seat. The church at Dura-Europos on the Euphrates has a raised platform on the east side of the assembly room, where we can presume that the chair for the service of the Word was placed. This was then replaced by a movable wooden altar for the Eucharist. Only with the expansion of the spaces for worship after the conversion of Constantine would the bishop have been as much as fifty yards distant from the last members of the audience, so that in order to be heard he had to advance to the front of the sanctuary. Thus from the end of the fourth century a podium had to be created for the lectors and for the preacher; they climbed up to it, and so it was called the "ambo," from Greek *anabainein,* "to go up." In Syria, a special form derived from the synagogue developed: the *bema* (rostrum), often placed in the exact middle of the church, in the midst of the congregation. It asserted itself as the central focus of the service of the Word, equal in importance to the altar and its surroundings. Here is the place of honor for the Scripture: There is a clear parallelism between this "table of the Word" and the altar, the corresponding "table of the Eucharistic gifts."

> The two poles of the Mass were set out in a manner that made them sensibly evident and impressive in their symbolism; they also corresponded in the most eminent manner with the Christian assembly for worship. . . . Would it not be possible to borrow from this basic conception in building new churches today? It would certainly not be misguided. Not only in new buildings with a central focus, but also in adapted historic churches and in naves with a long axis, we could take our lead from this concept in locating the axis between the ambo and the altar (J. H. Emminghaus).

At any rate, Western development proceeded in a different direction. The ritualization of the celebrations led to a division whereby the clerics were seated high up in the apse, and the choir of singers was placed on the *gradus,* the step of the ambo, (which is why the song between the readings is called the "gradual"). But the place for the proclamation of the Word was not firmly prescribed at any time; it was always regulated by expediency. This was true also for the development of rood screens and pulpits.

The place for proclamation has changed in the course of history, but its function was always key to the location: The Word of God should be understood by those who are gathered together. It was thus logical that monastic churches and cathedrals, where a large number of clerics prayed the Liturgy of the Hours, acquired a rood screen during the Middle Ages. It was not a question of putting up an iconostasis, as in the East, to veil the altar itself; rather it involved setting up a separate altar for the people, divided from the clerics' choir. The best place for proclamation of the Word was near this "altar of the cross" (so called because it was often surmounted with a cross flanked by figures of Mary and John); so the rood screen acquired a *lectorium* (place for reading aloud), our modern word "lectern." The development in parish churches was different: With the growth of preaching in the Middle Ages, and its increasing separation from the Eucharistic celebration, the ambo was removed still farther from the altar railing or rood screen into the body of the church. First there were wooden pulpits placed in the midst of the congregation, but since they were in the way of processions and other activities, they were later attached to the columns of the church. These are the pulpits one sees in medieval European churches today.

The basic principle behind this development is also decisive for the location of the ambo today: The reader must be visible and audible. Given the great variety of church layouts, it is impossible to prescribe exactly where the ambo should be placed; hence the statement in the introduction to the Lectionary, 32: "There must be a place in the church for the proclamation of God's Word, which is appropriate to the importance of that Word. . . . This place must be elevated, fixed and dignified. . . . In particular, it must make it easy for the congregation to listen attentively during the service of the Word." Thus, a special solution will be necessary for each individual church. The documents say nothing in detail about the form of the ambo, so that only the general prescription of The General Instruction of the Roman Missal (287; 312) applies: It should be of artistic quality and honorable simplicity; any material may be used "that by contemporary standards are considered to be of high quality, are durable, and well suited to sacred uses" (288). In addition, the church "strives . . . to promote new works of art that appeal to the contemporary mentality" (254).

It is probably wise to make the altar and the ambo of the same material.

The restrained decoration of the ambo should best be carried out within the limits of current iconography: symbols (e.g., the evangelists, the rivers of paradise) may possibly be preferable to human figures (Fathers of the Church, the sower, etc.). But care should be taken to remain within the realm of word-symbolism and not to make use of Eucharistic elements (lamb, pelican, etc.) (J. H. Emminghaus).

49

The Presider's Chair

According to The General Instruction of the Roman Missal, the priest's chair "ought to stand as a symbol of his office of presiding over the assembly and of directing it in prayer. Thus the best place for the chair is at the back of the sanctuary, and turned toward the congregation" (271).

Behind these instructions there is a clear basic direction toward the liturgical assembly and its duties. The presider has his place in relation to the other members of the presbytery, from which he leads the celebration. The person who has duties to perform at the two crystallization points of the service of the Word and the Eucharistic celebration, the ambo and the altar, goes first to the one place, then to the other. For the priest this means that he stands at the ambo to read the Gospel if there is no deacon to perform this duty, and he remains there for the homily and perhaps also for the petitions; he stands at the altar during the Eucharist. And that was essentially the order of things during the first millennium, an order that was interrupted at the point when private Masses replaced the one community Mass. At a private Mass "the celebrant stood at the altar from the beginning to the end of Mass and functioned there alone, except for a possible trip to the pulpit" (J. H. Emminghaus).

Originally the seat was seen as connected with the office: The one who wishes to be understood sits on an elevation, while the listeners stand or squat around her or him. Thus we read about Jesus that "he sat down, and his disciples came to him. And he opened his mouth and taught them" (Matt 5:1-2). So also the Christian bishop sat on his teaching chair, or *cathedra* (hence "cathedral" for a bishop's church), in front of the congregation. What at the beginning was a

155

simple chair at the rear wall of the apse became a throne in the fourth century, when bishops began to be state officials with senatorial rank. Only when bishops and priests began to turn their backs to the congregation while celebrating Mass was the altar pushed back to the wall of the apse and the *cathedra* placed on the gospel side. With the rise of private Masses around the year 1000, a chair for the priest became superfluous. The chairs in the choir were not seats for the presiders, since the priest and assistants sat there only during long periods of choral singing, in polyphonic Masses, for example.

> The chair for the presider, which is now to be restored, can in no way be modeled on the shape and placement of these seats: for the celebrant sat there only at those times when he was without function and disappeared from the picture! The renewed presider's chair, in contrast, should clearly emphasize his role during the Mass (J. H. Emminghaus).

Logically, in the new order of things the "back of the sanctuary" is again presumed to be the right place for the presider's chair, "unless the structure or other circumstances are an obstacle (for example, if too great a distance would interfere with communication between the priest and people)" (GIRM 271). This situation occurs especially in older churches with long, narrow choirs. But in principle it is certainly sensible for the presider to sit opposite the congregation and to exercise his or her functions there, as is the usual practice in secular assemblies. New buildings in the form of a square, a rhombus, a trapezoid, or some segment of a circle, however, offer the chance to place the presider's chair at the point envisioned by GIRM, without the priest's upper body being seen as if cut off by the altar. That today "anything resembling a throne is to be avoided" is probably a matter of course. While this presiding seat should probably be fixed in place, "the seats for the ministers should be so placed in the sanctuary that they can readily carry out their appointed functions" and can be arranged as necessary. Their placement should probably be chosen with a regard to expediency.

In any case we should maintain with Emminghaus that "the presider's chair is something new in modern awareness, and people in general do not yet fully grasp its meaning. An appropriately fashioned and functionally correct presider's chair could easily contribute to a better understanding and make it a normal part of the liturgy."

50

Reservation of the Eucharist

It is part of our renewed understanding of the Eucharist that the tabernacle should not be used for the distribution of Communion during the celebration of Mass (see ch. 32 above). For "the primary and original reason for reservation of the eucharist . . . is the administration of viaticum. The secondary reasons are the giving of communion and the adoration of our Lord Jesus Christ who is present in the sacrament" (introduction to *Holy Communion and Worship of the Eucharist Outside Mass*, 5). Adoration is thus only the consequence of the necessary reservation for the benefit of the sick and dying, for it "led to the praiseworthy practice of adoring this heavenly food in the churches." For this reason the consecrated hosts "are to be frequently renewed and reserved in a ciborium or other vessel, in a number sufficient for the Communion of the sick and others outside Mass" (7). If a community holds to these regulations, there should never be enough hosts in the tabernacle for the distribution of Communion during Mass.

But what should be the nature and appearance of the place for reservation of the Eucharist? According to The General Instruction of the Roman Missal (276), "Every encouragement should be given to the practice of Eucharistic reservation in a chapel suited to the faithful's private adoration and prayer." Only if this is "impossible because of the structure of the church, the sacrament should be reserved at an altar or elsewhere, in keeping with local custom, and in a part of the church that is worthy and properly adorned." And the introduction to the document on Eucharistic worship also "highly recommend[s]" a place that is suitable "for private adoration and prayer. . . . This will be achieved more easily if the chapel is separate from the body of the church" (9).

The place for the tabernacle is thus not a matter of free choice; it should, whenever possible, stand in a sacramental chapel separate from the main part of the church. Interestingly enough, nothing is said about an altar as the place for reservation. Only in the second sentence is permission conceded for placing the tabernacle on an altar in the body of the church—but not the principal altar—if reservation in a separate room is not possible. The authors were certainly thinking of old churches which have an ancient altar of historic and artistic value placed at the rear of the apse. The tabernacle can be placed on this altar, while Masses are celebrated at a separate, freestanding altar.

The new *Rite for the Dedication of Churches and Altars* also shows that a sacramental chapel is to be the normal place for Eucharistic reservation. There is a special rite given for the inauguration of the Blessed Sacrament chapel (79–82), which is to be celebrated after the concluding prayer of the Mass of Consecration, when transferring the Eucharist to the chapel. There is, however, no special ritual for consecrating the tabernacle. Perhaps we should keep in mind that the custom of giving a fixed place on the altar to the receptacle for reserving the Eucharist arose only at the end of the Middle Ages under the influence of Charles Borromeo (d. 1584). Only since then have the hosts been reserved neither in the sacristy, as in the earliest centuries, nor in the choir, as in the medieval period (hanging above the altar or standing on it in a small box, in a movable tabernacle, or in a sacramental tower). The direction that "as a rule there should be only one tabernacle in each church" (GIRM 277) is also important.

All these instructions make clear that the tabernacle is in no way designed for the reservation of the Eucharist for distribution during the celebration of Mass. Every community is thus called upon to consider how Communion can be distributed using bread and wine consecrated in the same Eucharistic celebration. Convenience should be no argument as regards the very center of the celebration of our faith.

ELEMENTARY SYMBOLS IN WORSHIP

51

The Easter Candle as Sensible Image of Christ

In German churches in the opening prayer for the Third Sunday of Easter the community prays: "Almighty God, let our Easter joy continue." One visible sign of this joy is the Easter candle, which stands throughout the Easter season next to the ambo from which the gospel, the light of the world, is proclaimed and which burns during every worship service. In the light service at the Easter Vigil, it is lighted from the new fire. Fire is the image of the love and power of the Spirit, as expressed in the hymn *Veni, Creator:* "Come, Holy Spirit, fill the hearts of thy faithful and enkindle in them the fire of thy love." Jesus has "come to cast fire on the earth; and would that it were already kindled!" (Luke 12:49). This fire took possession of the young Church; it is the image of Christ and, as tongues of fire, the image of his Holy Spirit. Therefore it is blessed at the Easter Vigil so that it may enkindle "in us the longing for you, the light that never fades."

In the Middle Ages it was the custom to extinguish all lights and fires in order to begin a new life in each house with the Easter fire. A cross and the number of the year, together with the letters A and Ω, are incised in the Easter candle. The text to be spoken while doing this says: "Christ yesterday and today (vertical arm), the beginning and the end (horizontal arm), Alpha and Omega. All time belongs to him (first numeral), and all the ages (second numeral). To him be glory and power (third numeral) through every age for ever (fourth numeral). Amen." Five grains of incense may represent Jesus' wounds. The lighting of the candle from the fire is accompanied by the words "May the light of Christ, rising in glory, dispel the darkness of our hearts and minds."

The Easter candle is carried in procession into the darkened church, accompanied by the proclamation: "The light of Christ," or "Christ our light," to which the congregation responds in song: "Thanks be to God." Gradually the candles held by all present are lighted from the Easter candle. The great Easter song of praise (Exultet) is a tribute to the light that God gives the community (see ch. 37 above): "Darkness vanishes for ever," for "of this night Scripture says: 'the night will be as clear as day: it will become my light, my joy.' " It "casts out hatred, brings us peace, and humbles earthly pride. . . . Father, in the joy of this night, receive our evening sacrifice of praise, . . . Accept this Easter candle. . . ." At the blessing of the baptismal water it can be lowered into the font, something that used to be necessary in the great baptistries so that one could see: "We ask you, Father, with your Son, to send the Holy Spirit upon the waters of this font." The candle is in this way an image of Christ, the "true light that enlightens everyone" (John 1:9). This light remains with us. Therefore it is no longer extinguished on Ascension Thursday, as it used to be. Only after Pentecost is the candle carried from the ambo to the baptismal font (see ch. 22 above), where it is advisable to have it burning during all worship services.

The ways in which the Easter candle may be connected to the liturgy outside the Easter season depend on the location of the baptismal font in any given church. The liturgical books, other than the Missal, give only two indications, namely in *The Rite for the Baptism of Children,* according to which it can be lighted for the baptism and the candles of those being baptized may be lighted from it, and in *The Rite for Christian Burial,* which says that the burning Easter candle may stand at the head of the deceased during the funeral Mass. If both aspects are to be combined the baptismal font must be within view of the congregation, in or near the sanctuary so that the Easter candle, while removed from the ambo, still remains visible to the assembly. If necessary, it will have to be carried from the baptismal font to the place where the funeral Mass is celebrated. In any case it should be "set up in an easily visible place, in order to make evident the connection between the baptism, death, and resurrection of the faithful and the resurrection of Christ," as the German introduction to *The Rite of Funerals* (32) indicates.

Since it is precisely this connection, so wonderfully symbolized by the Easter candle, that is at issue, it could also be expressed in other liturgical celebrations: for example, when candles are blessed and carried in procession at the Feast of Candlemas, by lighting them at the Easter candle placed in the sanctuary; or by carrying the light from the Easter candle to the graves on the Feast of All Saints or All Souls; or by lighting the Advent wreath and the Christmas candles from the Easter candle. Much more important, however, is the inclusion of the Easter candle in the celebration of First Communion (see ch. 25 above), its use for lighting the bridal candle or the candles of the newly ordained, and certainly for the wake service celebrated by the community or neighbors between death and burial. On Sunday also, the connection between the annual paschal feast at Easter and the weekly Pasch of the Sunday Eucharist could be made evident, perhaps by lighting the two candles which are carried in the gospel procession from the Easter candle.

All these questions about the symbolism of the Easter candle in liturgical celebrations can certainly be answered only in and from the individual situation of a particular community. However, a word about Lent is in order. Here, corresponding to the silencing of the Alleluia on Ash Wednesday, a "fasting of the ears," there could be a parallel "fasting of the eyes" emphasized by not burning the Easter candle during the period of Quadragesima (cf. the covering of images and crucifix on the Fifth Sunday of Lent). Of course, even in Lent, every Sunday is an Easter celebration. There does not seem to be any ready-made solution possible, but this might be one possible way of proceeding.

It would also make sense to give a particular form to the removal of the Easter candle on Pentecost Sunday. Hermann Reifenberg calls for a procession from the ambo to the baptismal font before the solemn blessing and suggests the possibility also of a service of the Word, perhaps in connection with Pentecost Vespers.

52

"Nongenuine" Candles?

There are some churches here and there that use imitation candles instead of real ones on the altar: The shaft is made of a permanent material, and at the top is a space in which small warmer candles can be inserted. There are also electric vigil lights: Put in a quarter, press a button, and the electric bulb "burns" for a determined length of time. What can we say about this kind of "symbolism"?

The foreword to the prayer of blessing for candles in the Benedictional says: "Even for us in our technical age, burning candles are a sign of joy and hope, of prayer and sacrifice; we see ourselves reflected in them. They remind us at the same time that Christ called himself the light of the world and urged us to live as children of light." A candle is thus a symbol of Christ and reminds us of the burning lights in the hands of the vigilant virgins (see Matt 25:1-12). That is why we use burning candles in the gospel procession, at the entrance of the newly baptized and first communicants, and that is probably why we place candles on the altar (although they have only been distributed all over the altar since the fourteenth century).

Today "on or near the altar there are to be candlesticks with lighted candles, at least two but even four, six or, if the bishop of the diocese celebrates, seven"—probably a reflection of Rev 1:12 (GIRM 79). These are "a sign of reverence and festiveness" (GIRM 269). "The places and requisites for worship should be truly worthy and beautiful, signs and symbols of heavenly realities" (GIRM 253). Therefore "the choice of materials for church appointments must be marked by concern for genuineness and by the intent to foster instruction of the faithful and the dignity of the place of worship" (GIRM 279).

These few excerpts from the Missal already furnish an answer to the question raised above and to the remarkable practices that seem to be creeping in here and there, especially in other countries. In an interpretation of these remarks as early as 1974, the Congregation for Divine Worship determined that there are clear regulations only for the so-called eternal light at the tabernacle, according to which this lamp should be fed by oil or wax; for all other candles, as for every liturgical object, the bishops' conferences can choose suitable materials. But the statement continues: "Candles intended for liturgical use should be made of a material that produces a steady flame and does not produce smoke or a bad odor nor soil the cloths and carpets. For the sake of authenticity, and to obtain a clearer meaning for the light, no electric candles should be used." At the beginning of 1986 the Catholic bishops of England and Wales decided that the use of electric "candles" was unacceptable. Oil-filled imitation candles were also rejected, for, according to the bishops, "liturgical celebrations should be marked by truth and authenticity." The liturgical commission of the U.S. bishops' conference also issued a similar declaration a few years ago. According to this paper, the use of any material other than wax for the production of candles is not permitted. The text reads:

> at the celebration of Mass and at other liturgical celebrations, candles made from wax must be used. In addition, because of their unique place in the liturgy, imitations of candles are not to be used, for example as permanent Easter candles. Nor should electric bulbs be used. In the interests of genuineness and symbolic content, it is also most inappropriate to use so-called electric vigil lights for purposes of veneration.

This really needs no augmentation. One may continue to hope that a similar declaration will not even be necessary in German-speaking countries. How can we, on the one hand, complain about a supposed reduction of symbols in our renewed liturgy and, on the other hand, replace the symbols with sham objects (see ch. 15 above)? A reference to our technical age is no argument, for there has probably never been a time when so many candles were used for private purposes as there are today.

53

What Does Incense Symbolize?

More incense is being used in solemn liturgies today than was the case just a few years ago. But nobody seems clear about whether there are rules for its use: what or who should be incensed, and what meaning the use of incense can have today, if any.

One needs only to thumb through an old book of rubrics to see what a complicated set of rules formerly existed: who or what was to be incensed with one, two, or three "swings" and "circles." By contrast, the present rule is simply: "The use of incense is optional in any form of Mass" (GIRM 235). Occasions within the liturgy include the entrance procession; the beginning of the Mass (incensing the altar); the gospel procession and proclamation; the preparation of the gifts (gifts, altar, priest, and people are incensed); when host and chalice are shown to the people after the consecration. There is no binding rule that incense is always to be used at each of these moments. The Benedictional describes the meaning of incense thus: It "is in particular an expression of festival joy and solemn prayer." And at the dedication of an altar, when grains of incense are burned on the altar the bishop says: "Lord, may our prayer ascend as incense in your sight. As this building is filled with fragrance so may your Church fill the world with the fragrance of Christ." Since in the imperial cult of late antiquity incense served as a sign of divine honor given to the emperor and thus meant a falling-away from Christian faith, it was used by Christians only at burials (to drive away the smell of decay) and for refreshment; it appears in the Western liturgy only since the time of Charlemagne, mainly due to the influence of Old Testament motifs (e.g., Exod 13:21: "The Lord went before them in a pillar of cloud by day"; Ps 141:2, "May my prayer come before you like incense").

The oldest liturgical use of incense of which we have witness was at the reading of the Gospel, first as an honor to Christ the Lord, and then as an image of the fragrance of his teaching. The altar, the book of the Gospels, and the Eucharist have always been the "signs of the Lord present in the Eucharistic celebration, who is honored as *Kyrios* through the smoke of the incense" (B. Kleinheyer).

The incensing at the preparation of the gifts does not seem to fit into this, which is why The General Instruction of the Roman Missal gives a special reason for it (51): "This is a symbol of the Church's offering and prayer going up to God. Afterward the deacon or other minister may incense the priest and the people." It is not a matter of honor paid to the gifts or to persons, but a sign of participation in the sacrifice for which the community is preparing itself:

> We ourselves are gifts offered to God; the ascending incense is an image of our own self-surrender. Therefore it would be contrary to the intended meaning if the congregation were to remain seated during the incensation. They should, in any case, be standing for the prayer over the gifts. When the congregation stands for the incensation, it is a sign that we are raising ourselves up, because our hearts are directed upward, like the incense rising to heaven (B. Kleinheyer).

The celebrant used to say, when handing over the censer, "May the Lord kindle in us the fire of surrender, the flame of abiding love." Our lives should be brought before the face of God as divine praise. This expression has been omitted because during the singing it would remain inaudible to the congregation. Therefore, the meaning of the rite needs to be explained to the community from time to time. Romano Guardini explained the rising fragrance as follows: "In the rhythm and the sweetness there is a musical quality; and like music also is the entire lack of practical utility: It is a prodigal waste of precious material. It is a pouring out of unwithholding love. . . . It is as free and objectless as beauty. It burns and is consumed like love that lasts through death." For Balthasar Fischer it is "a symbol of that atmosphere of prayer evoked by the ancient cry of the presider at the threshold of the Eucharistic celebration's central moment: *Sur-*

sum corda—Lift up your hearts. . . . No symbol can represent the upward movement so simply and so effectively as incense.''

When persons are incensed at the preparation of the gifts, they do not come first, but only after the incensing of the gifts and the altar. It is by no means a matter of giving honor to persons, for incense is always a sign of honor given to the Lord present in the Eucharistic celebration, especially in the altar, the Gospel book, and the Eucharistic gifts. But, when the celebrant and the congregation are also incensed, even though this is done after the gifts and the altar are incensed, it may awaken misunderstandings today, since it reminds us of former times when incensing was really interpreted as giving honor to persons, "when every cleric in the choir was incensed, and in cathedral churches a fine distinction was made as to who received incense once, twice, or three times" (B. Kleinheyer).

It seems to be unclear in many places as well what one ought to do with the censer. The Roman Congregation for Divine Worship answered a question on this topic in 1976, because there are no details given in the Missal. They speak of "three swings" at every incensation. The circular motions that used to be made are no longer mentioned. Prayers are no longer used, neither while placing incense in the censer nor during the incensation itself. Incidentally, one should walk around the altar while incensing it. If the altar is not separated from the wall, the right side is to be incensed first, then the left. If the crucifix stands on or near the altar, it is to be incensed first; if it is behind the altar, it is incensed by the priest when he walks by it.

It appears to be important that the altar servers hold the censer steady at other times. If it is constantly swinging, so that incense is always ascending, the symbol no longer expresses what it is supposed to. The fact that there are no longer detailed instructions for all this corresponds to a changed understanding of liturgy, which, however, calls as always for thoughtful consideration of the question of what is appropriate in order to make clear what a particular symbol intends to express.

Undoubtedly, there are other ways of making this symbol "speak" more clearly. For example, young people have immediate access to it if—something that is best done in smaller groups—the censer is not swung but placed before the altar so that all participants have a chance to place incense on the burning coals; this is done very quietly while, during this meditative silence for offering incense, the "incense psalm" (Ps 141) can be sung: "Let my prayer come before you like incense, my Lord and my God." This is most appropriate at the Liturgy of the Hours, for example, before the Magnificat at Vespers.

Thus it is worthwhile to give some thought to the language spoken by old, seemingly worn-out signs in the liturgy today. It should go without saying that the sense of smell should not be insulted by inappropriate mixtures of odors. Only a pleasant smell can express the symbolism that is sought after.

54

The Gospel Book as Symbol of the Word of God

For some time now we have had a special Gospel Lectionary from which to proclaim the Gospel. In the introduction to the Lectionary (36) we read:

> Since the proclamation of the Gospel has always been the climax of the service of the Word, the liturgies of East and West have agreed in differentiating the books used for the various readings. The book containing the Gospels was prepared and decorated with even greater care, and was more highly venerated than any other book of biblical readings.

In any event, the Roman liturgy, unlike those of the East, had abandoned this special symbol of the presence of the Lord in his Word, because the priest alone took all the parts in the worship service, with the result that the complete Missal became the all-purpose book. Only now that the community has recovered its liturgical office in the last few years have we begun to have liturgical books for the various roles. So the Lectionary, with all the readings and Gospels, was produced for the use of the lector, deacon, and priest. But, as was always the case in the Byzantine liturgy, the Gospel book should serve to make even clearer that the Lord himself enters into the midst of his community. In the Gospel book the Lord himself is venerated and the mystery of his presence is symbolically emphasized.

"Since the publication of the German Gospel book our congregations have the opportunity to develop the decayed rituals anew and to bring the Gospel element to a new level of awareness, with the symbol of the Gospel book forming the climax, both verbal and nonverbal, of the Liturgy of the Word" (F. Kohlschein). It should be carried in the entrance procession and laid on the altar (which, of course, should not be a parking place for all sorts of things and, at this point, should not even contain the Missal or chalice). Before the proclamation of the Gospel, the Gospel book is then carried by the deacon or priest in solemn procession, with candles and incense, to the ambo. Consideration could certainly be given to a major procession, for during it the Gospel acclamation is to be sung by the congregation. The importance of the Gospel could also be emphasized if, as in the East, it were sung. The way we treat the Gospel book should correspond at all times to the importance of this symbol: It can remain lying on the ambo or, as in the East, be returned to rest on the altar; if there is no fixed place for it in the sanctuary, it must be carried out again at the recessional. The older Lectionary will still be used for the other readings. It could lie on the credence table; the lector would take it from there and return it after the readings.

The symbolic importance of the Gospel book is similar to that of the Eucharistic species.

> In the churches where a tabernacle in the choir emphasizes the dignity of the Eucharistic gifts, the visible symbol of the Word could be an important addition. The consciousness of the dignity of the Word of God is of the utmost pastoral urgency today; it must be awakened from its centuries-long disappearance into oblivion. . . . Every symbolic action in the liturgy should prepare the climate in which the Word of God can become active in our hearts and evoke action. Liturgical veneration of the Gospel book is not rooted in magical ideas but in the conviction of the revealing rule of God in Christ. Through a worthy symbolic relationship to the Gospel book, a community can be prepared and awakened for the Easter event of salvation in the proclaimed Word of the exalted Lord (F. Kohlschein).

A distinction should be made between keeping the Gospel book in the sanctuary and having a Bible there; the latter should be available for the use of those who visit the church, but the focus is not on its symbolic meaning.

55

Liturgical Books as Expressions of Our Concept of Liturgy

If the Church must constantly reform itself *(ecclesia semper reformanda)*, then the liturgy that celebrates the faith of the Church must also be constantly reformed *(liturgia semper reformanda)*. Thus the current liturgical books are always a reflection of the state of liturgical consciousness of a given period.

A glance at the history of the Church shows that liturgy has never really stood still. An altered understanding of the faith has always brought with it a change in the expression of that faith in worship, which means changes in the liturgy. Even the Roman Missal of 1570, which was replaced by the Missal of Paul VI in 1970, did not survive those four centuries—a "period of rubricism and of iron unified lockstep in liturgy" (T. Klauser)—totally unchanged. This is even more true of the other liturgical ceremonies, such as the sacraments, which were often celebrated in different ways even from diocese to diocese down into the twentieth century.

As long as Latin was the only liturgical language, adaptations at least at the level of speech were scarcely demanded, since Latin never changed. But we can see from looking at the developments in biblical translation that adaptations were, in fact, necessary at certain intervals. And that in itself, of course, affected the liturgy: We are already using the second Lectionary to be prepared since the introduction of the vernacular liturgy, because the Common Translation *(Einheits über-setzung)* has become standard in Germany, just as the New American

Bible has come into use in the United States. This in turn called for changes in the liturgical books, since many liturgical texts are based on passages from Scripture.

Or to take another example: The New Code of Canon Law of 1983 required the revamping of many liturgical celebrations. These changes were collected in the *Variationes. Changes in the Liturgical Books* (AAS 58). Earlier, Roman standard books were usually translated for our region, generally without major adaptations to conditions here, although such adaptations were desired by the Council. The practice of the last several years has yielded a good many justified requests that make a revision appear sensible. But Rome has also prepared new versions of a number of ceremonies in the last few years, not least because of the progress of theological research. Beyond this, there are several liturgical books that, two decades after the Council, have still not been issued, in most cases because fundamental research remains to be done—for example, the so-called *Great Exorcism,* a "liturgy for delivery from evil spirits," for which there are still medical and psychotherapeutic questions to be resolved. Many books have only appeared in German-speaking countries as drafts, because it was seen that a period of testing was needed before they could be formally introduced, for example, *The Rite of Penance* or *The Rite for Christian Initiation of Adults.* Since 1975 there have been a number of additions and changes to the Missal worldwide; these still need to be integrated. And *The Rite of Marriage* still lags far behind modern demands; it does not even envision the marriage of partners from differing confessions. As regards *The Pastoral Care of the Sick* also, there have been a number of requests, especially from those practically engaged in the care of the sick; these are now being incorporated. Something similar can be said for the German Benedictional, which exists only in a draft dating from 1977; in the meantime a worldwide edition has been produced in Rome, which will require changes in the German liturgical books. And in the long term there will always be at least minor liturgical changes to express the changes in belief and in our perception of the liturgy.

But the form of the liturgical books themselves is a sign of changing views of liturgy. In a time when only clerics were seen as capable of doing liturgy there was no need for liturgical books for the congregation, not even for those filling other roles in the liturgy, because a ceremony was regarded as validly performed only when every word from beginning to end was spoken by the priest. Therefore the Roman Missal of 1570 was a so-called complete Missal, containing all the texts that are pronounced in any Mass, since the celebrating priest had to speak all of them. In contrast, the postconciliar Missal of 1970 contains only those texts that are to be spoken by the one presiding at the Eucharistic celebration, especially the orations and the Eucharistic prayer. The scriptural readings are in the Lectionary, the lector's book. There is a cantor's book for the cantor, and the congregation's book, in Germany, is *Gotteslob* (the common collection of prayers and hymns, with special sections for the different diocesan editions). Thus books for the various roles have taken the place of the complete Missal. This expresses the fact that the whole community and all those who serve it are the actors in the liturgy, and not only the priest.

56

The Hunger Cloth— Revival of a Lost Symbol

Even in the early Middle Ages in many churches people began to drape cloths over the altars, with their statues and pictures, crosses, carvings, and reliquaries in order to relegate these beautiful objects to the background during the penitential season. A simplification of church decoration as a whole went hand in hand with this movement. One possible reason was the solidarity of the faithful with those doing public penance, who were expelled from the church at the beginning of Lent. But since all the people were conscious that they were one with the penitents in being sinners, the whole congregation wanted to deny itself the view of the altar. This was referred to as a "fasting of the eyes." As a substitute for the covered pictures, the cloths themselves were decorated in many places in the course of time with pictorial representations, especially those related to the Passion of Christ. This custom was elevated to the status of liturgical law in the Missal of 1570: "Before Vespers on the first Sunday of the Passion the crucifixes and images are covered." The new order of the Roman liturgy has made this custom optional and placed it at the discretion of the bishops' conferences, thus making it subject to local tradition. The new German Missal directs for the Fifth Sunday of Lent, which has replaced Passion Sunday: "The custom of covering the crucifixes and images in churches should be retained. In this case the crucifixes remain covered until the end of the Good Friday liturgy, and the images until the beginning of the Easter Vigil." The custom is thus no longer obligatory in our country. But when it is done, it

175

would make good sense to cover only the images and crucifixes that represent the Lord enthroned in glory, not those that show him in his humiliation.

The so-called hunger cloth, which seems to have appeared at the same time as the custom of swathing the images and which is witnessed at least from the year 1000, covered the whole sanctuary. It was first used in monastic and cathedral churches to separate the sanctuary from the choir; later it appeared in parish churches to divide the sanctuary from the nave. Thus the hunger cloth became a sign of the Church's fasting; it was also called a "fasting sheet" or "languishing rag" *(Schmachtlappen)*. The expression "to gnaw on the hunger cloth" probably stems from this. Since the fifteenth century it has gradually disappeared, as it was replaced by popular pictures of the Passion, Lenten tableaux, and scenes of the Mount of Olives, but especially by the stations of the cross.

The *Misereor* collection for the Third World, which is taken up among German Catholics during Lent, led in the mid-1970s to an effort to visualize the event in connection with the Lenten fast. For this purpose, the forgotten custom of the hunger cloth was revived, with images taken from the churches and cultures of the Third World in order to make these visually present for Westerners. Thus an old liturgical custom was rediscovered for the contemporary world. The first assignment to produce a hunger cloth went to an Indian artist, the second to an Ethiopian. It was to thematize the idea of the human being as God's creature in a world where goods are unevenly distributed and in which the salvation of all can only be achieved if the rich share their wealth with the poor. Its success was astonishing; in a very short time two-thirds of all Catholic parishes were involved. Copies were also ordered by a large number of Lutheran parishes in the first year. Since then a smaller version has been produced for home use.

In this way an unexpected revival of the custom of the hunger cloth has been achieved in German-speaking countries. Its consequences for Church life were equally beyond expectation. Moreover, it has enriched the liturgy and has shown that even in our time new symbols can be created or buried symbols revived. There is, however, a precondition for such an event, namely, that it find a genuine home in our Christian communities.

57

Liturgical Vestments: Expressive Symbols

Liturgical clothing (vestments) developed out of the desire to don special garments for worship. At first they were no different from everyday clothing. Only when clerics were given the rank of state officials under emperor Constantine did they also receive the right to wear the insignia of office and the garments that were reserved for the higher social orders. After the barbarian invasions, liturgical vestments differing from everyday wear were adopted. Clerics kept the old Roman garb for worship, but also for every day: a long undergarment (tunic) and another garment over it (toga); the alb and chasuble developed from these. In the Middle Ages under the influence of Old Testament precedents, these vestments acquired a hierarchical character: The individual garments were blessed, given allegorical meanings, and special prayers were said while putting them on. The bishop in particular was solemnly vested.

Probably no one today will dispute the fact that every major solemn community gathering calls for the officeholders to wear special clothing as a sign of their office. Even the Reformation, which abolished everything that the medieval mind regarded as priestly clothing, retained at least a long robe. Liturgical vestments should distinguish those who perform a special service: The presider should be recognizable as such, and the service being performed should overshadow the individual performing it. For this purpose there is no particular need for splendid vestments.

The General Instruction on the Roman Missal also presumes that the multiplicity of services should be expressed by a variety of vestments (297–310). For the celebration of Mass, the priest wears a chasuble over alb and stole. This chasuble, which originally was an overcoat for bad weather and then in the fourth century became a garment for solemn occasions, was taken over by clerics as a robe of office and, in the West, has been worn only for celebrating Mass since about the year 1000. Previously these chasubles were splendidly decorated, and such vestments may still be in use here and there. But "the beauty of a liturgical vestment should derive from its material and design rather than from lavish ornamentation" (GIRM 306). In addition, "the conference of bishops may choose and propose to the Apostolic See adaptations suited to the needs and culture of peoples" (GIRM 308). The Austrian bishops did this in the early 1970s, permitting as a substitute for alb, stole, and chasuble a vestment that eliminates the duplication of liturgical under- and outer-garment (alb and chasuble) and that can be worn as the only liturgical vestment, together with the stole, over the everyday clothing. In other places as well, a robe with sleeves is worn, which covers the body and so makes the alb as undergarment superfluous. This coat-type vestment is usually light in weight and unchanging in color; the liturgical colors are represented by the stole which is worn over it. Since this robe can also be worn by bishops and deacons, it fulfills the desire for a simple standard.

The need for such a symbol certainly depends on the size of the assembly. The smaller the group assembled for the liturgy, the more likely it is that one can do without it. Accordingly, the "German Bishops' Conference Regulations for Masses Celebrated in Smaller Assemblies (Group Masses)" of September 24, 1970, orders that "the clothing, posture, and gestures of the participants" must "be appropriate to the dignity of divine worship." In this context

> the priest's clothing serves to emphasize the service of the priest, who represents Christ within the community and presides over the celebration. Thus even in Masses celebrated in smaller groups it is not appropriate to forego a mode of dress adapted to worship services or to do without liturgical symbols. . . . In unusual cases the priest may be adequately designated (if he is vested) as prescribed for the administration of other sacraments, but it goes without saying that the stole may never be omitted.

There is much to be said also for wearing appropriate clothing for the performance of other services in the liturgy. Thus the liturgical instruction *Holy Communion and Worship of the Eucharist Outside Mass* says of the dress of those who assist in distributing Communion: "Other ministers should wear either the liturgical vesture which may be traditional in their region or the vestment which is appropriate for this ministry and has been approved by the Ordinary" (20). There are also good practical reasons for this, since a light summer dress may, for example, not be suitable for this service, and in the winter the minister need not wear a heavy coat.

Undoubtedly, liturgical vestments represent a thoroughly secondary form of symbol. Every individual community will have to find its own way in this matter.

58

Green or White on Sundays?

The liturgical colors, like vestments, can only claim a thoroughly secondary type of symbolism. For example, one might ask why green should be the liturgical color for the Sundays in Ordinary Time. It is true that the Sunday Eucharistic celebration has a special relationship to Easter; it is the community's weekly reminder of Easter, and so one could well ask whether the paschal character of the day would not better be represented by white. What were the considerations that led to the adoption of green in the new order of the liturgy?

Probably there was no especially deep thought given to the matter, since The General Instruction of the Roman Missal says: "Traditional usage should be retained for the vestment colors" (308). And that means that green is still prescribed for the Sundays in Ordinary Time and white for the Easter and Christmas seasons as well as for certain feasts. But this has only been "traditional usage" since 1570. From a historical point of view, it was in the Carolingian Period that (in some places) it became customary to designate a color for liturgical vestments that seemed appropriate for certain feasts. Only at the beginning of the thirteenth century was a canon of colors introduced by Pope Innocent III, but it was not yet obligatory.

Such a fixed set of colors could only come into being when people began to interpret the celebrations allegorically, even as a species of parables (see ch. 15 above). The next step was to give meaning to the colors: red as the color of blood for the martyrs, violet as the color of penance, black as the color of mourning. Originally, the outer garments were colored according to status, wealth, and solemnity. Dying was done by boiling the fabric in diluted secretions of the Murex snail. Depending on the quantity of the extremely expensive dye, tones ranging from rose through red, green to violet, and the especially expensive black were obtained. Ancient Christian mosaics therefore show bishops in dark purple tones, deacons more usually in white. So anyone who could afford it wore black on festival days, and it remains the color for men's formal dress even now. As a color of mourning also, black is really a ceremonial color. With the decline of ancient culture, the technique and knowledge of purple dying were lost. Use of vegetable dyes then led to a new symbolization in the Middle Ages. Red and gold were seen as colors of the sun and were appropriated to God the Father and to the king; blue, as the color of the sky, was only for Christ and Mary; green as the color of the meadow, the forest, and the creation was for the Holy Spirit but also for the apostles as bearers of the Spirit and for bishops. Thus bishops who were not noblemen at least of the rank of count wore green up to the year 1803.

Seen from this point of view, any scheme of colors for the liturgy today is certainly questionable in the best sense of the word. If the Sundays in Ordinary Time were to be distinguished by white, as are the Sundays of Easter and Christmas, then why not the Sundays in Lent as well? These, too, are memorials of the resurrection of the Lord and have a clearly paschal character. And in fact, this suggestion is worthy of consideration. If we take the paschal nature of these Sundays seriously, white could certainly be the color for every Sunday.

In any case, The General Instruction of the Roman Missal offers an opening, since "on solemn occasions more precious vestments may be used, even if not of the color of the day" (309); also, the bishops' conferences may "choose and propose to the Apostolic See adaptations suited to the needs and culture of peoples" (308). The fact that this is not a question of central importance is clear from the usage of the Eastern Church, which even today has no fixed list of liturgical colors. On the other hand, colors have a strong expressive value for human beings, so that it is worth giving some thought to the way they are used. But liturgical colors are by no means an essential symbol.

59

"Remember that you are dust": The Symbol of Ashes

As early as the beginning of the Middle Ages, the penitential season began with the Wednesday before the First Sunday of Lent (Ash Wednesday). The penitents received their robe of sackcloth and, at an early stage, were also strewn with ashes. Both symbols were known in the Old Testament and in antiquity as expressions of mourning and of a penitential spirit. Jesus speaks of them in his lament over Chorazin and Bethsaida: "If the mighty works done in you had been done in Tyre and Sidon, they would have repented long ago in sackcloth and ashes" (Matt 11:21). When public penance (see ch. 33 above) ceased to be practiced, the custom arose of dispensing ashes in the context of a penitential liturgy for all the faithful; this is known first from the end of the eleventh century. Something that had meaning within the penitential liturgy became problematic by the end of the Middle Ages, when the blessing of ashes was separated from the service and the blessed ashes began to be seen as something holy. They were then used as a protection against headaches or spread over gardens and fields. The renewed liturgy retains the distribution of ashes but contextualizes it firmly in the notion of penance, which is quite right, since Ash Wednesday is to be kept as a day of fasting.

The blessing of the ashes takes place after the Gospel and homily. A choice of two prayers is offered, with the petition that we may "keep this lenten season in preparation for the joy of Easter." To this same end we ask in the second oration that God "keep us faithful to the discipline of Lent" that we may "live with the risen Christ, who reigns

. . . for ever and ever." In only one of the prayers does it say that we are marked with ashes, "by which we show that we are dust." It is evident that not everyone responsible for the liturgy found this note, which recalls the expulsion from Paradise (see Gen 3:19), appropriate for the day, since for the signing with ashes an alternative phrase is suggested: "Turn away from sin and be faithful to the Gospel"—Jesus' cry at his first appearance in Galilee according to Mark 1:15. And during the placing of the cross of ashes, antiphons are suggested that speak only of conversion and not of mortality.

It is certainly appropriate that the prayer for salvation should be uttered at the beginning of Lent, as in the penitential Ps 51: "According to thy abundant mercy blot out my transgressions!" The scriptural texts do not speak of mortality but of repentance and reconciliation, while the Gospel, drawn from the Sermon on the Mount, talks of almsgiving, prayer, and fasting, all of which must be done in the right spirit (see Joel 2:12-18; 2 Cor 5:20–6:2; Matt 6:1-6, 16-18). Certainly the giving of ashes should be explained to the community in the homily. Ashes are not only a sign of mortality but also of cleansing. Soap used to be made from ashes. And when the words "Remember that you are dust" are interpreted as a sign of penance, as a reference to mortality (if we do not repent in order to be properly prepared to celebrate Easter), good use can be made of the symbol of ashes in harmony with the responsory suggested for use during the distribution of ashes: "Direct our hearts to better things, O Lord; heal our sin and ignorance. Lord, do not face us suddenly with death, but give us time to repent."

Thus the symbol of ashes is not a contradiction to the preparation for Easter; with its reference to mortality and to purification it is, in itself, a sign of that preparation.